From Deacon to Man of God!

From Deacon to Man of God!

A Guide for Latter-day Saint Young Men
Twelve to Eighteen Years Old

By Rulon Dean Skinner

Horizon Publishers
Springville, Utah

ISBN: 0-88290-799-9
e. 1
Order Number: C3006

Published by Horizon Publishers,
an imprint of Cedar Fort, Inc.
925 N. Main, Springville, Utah, 84663
www.cedarfort.com
Distributed by:

Cover design by Nicole Williams
Cover design © 2006 by Lyle Mortimer
Printed in the United States of America

10 9 8 7 6 5 4 3 2 1

Printed on acid-free paper

Contents

Dedication

This book is dedicated to the missionaries of The Church of Jesus Christ of Latter-day Saints. I love each one of them. Each is an inspiration to me. I thrill with the opportunity I have had to serve in a branch presidency at the Missionary Training Center in Provo for eight and a half years (two callings). I often would tell the new missionaries, "I love the MTC for two reasons: (1) the quality of young missionaries who come to the MTC dedicated to serve Heavenly Father and Jesus Christ with all their heart, soul, and mind; (2) the Holy Ghost is always present and can be felt at the MTC." I appreciate and cherish the many opportunities I have had since my second release from a branch presidency to return and assist a current branch presidency.

Each new missionary arrives at the MTC at a different level of premission preparation. A large majority of missionaries have been members since eight years of age; others have been members just a year or two. Missionaries come from strong Church families; others are the only member of the Church in their family. Missionaries come from two-parent families; others come from single-parent families. Some have been working and saving for their missions; others have no financial resources for their mission. Almost all new missionaries have cleared past sins with their bishops and not repeated the sins since repenting; others have not been 100 percent truthful with their bishops. Missionaries arrive at the MTC who have read the Book of Mormon at least once, while others have not. Most missionaries come with a testimony; others only believe. Most missionaries are on their missions because they want to be; some feel pressured by family, the ward, or friends.

Some of the basic things they need to learn at the MTC include obeying the mission rules (Missionary Handbook) and serving with quiet dignity (representing the Savior the way they should by how they dress, what they do or don't do, what they say or don't say). Missionaries must also learn to love their companions, to work hard, to live and teach with the Spirit, to be sure they have fully repented of past sins and are worthy to have the Holy Ghost as their companion, to learn a new language (if called to a mission with a new language), to learn the doctrine—Heavenly Father's plan of happiness for his children and the gospel of Jesus Christ—to take care of personal needs (laundry, personal hygiene, health, and so forth), and to use time wisely to accomplish all these things.

As they work on the things listed above and master them, they get more excited about their missions and time seems to go by fast. They can hardly wait to get into the mission field and share the news of Heavenly Father's plan of happiness for his children. They are eager to bring people to Christ.

Thus, I would like to dedicate *From Deacon to Man of*

God! to the missionaries of The Church of Jesus Christ of Latter-day Saints.

Preface

It is my hope that this book will inspire and challenge young men to seriously prepare during their Aaronic Priesthood years for a mission, temple marriage, and fatherhood. They can best prepare for these things by becoming men of God by the time they receive the Melchizedek Priesthood.

I realize the key role the father in the Church must play if his son is to make the proper transition during his Aaronic Priesthood years. Preparation must begin almost from birth. In this book, I focus on the preparation that begins when a young man is twelve years old and continues until he receives the Melchizedek Priesthood. If the young man sees himself as a man of God, the process will continue through his adult years.

Although this book is written to young men, it is important and vital that parents read it before or at the same time their son does. Mothers must not be left out of this preparation. This book will help parents realize their important role in their son's preparation, as well as his overall growth from boy to man, and they will be in a better position to be supportive, make suggestions, guide, and teach their son. They will see the fruits of their labors as he performs his priesthood duties, serves a mission, marries in the temple, and becomes a worthy husband and father.

It is assumed that the young man has been born into an active, priesthood-led family. If this is not the case, then appropriate adjustments must be made for the young man to make the transition from deacon to man of God. Some of these adjustments have been suggested in this book.

By making the transition from deacon to man of God, young men will have truly taken upon themselves Christ as their Savior, Redeemer, and God. They will be struggling daily to become more Christlike and to have the Holy Ghost as their constant companion. They will realize life's greatest joys come in service to others. Indeed, they will understand King Benjamin's statement: "And behold, I tell you these things that ye may learn wisdom; that ye may learn that when ye are in the service of your fellow beings ye are only in the service of your God" (Mosiah 2:17). They will be happy. They will be at peace with themselves and with God.

This book is intended to be a guide for Latter-day Saint young men twelve to eighteen years of age. It does not address all the issues that contribute to the transition from boy to man, but it does contain valuable instructions that, if followed, will put them far ahead of young men who do not apply these instructions to their lives.

It is my suggestion that when you receive this book, regardless of your age, read it cover to cover as quickly as you can. Then once you have a feel for the entire book, go through it again and decide which chapters you are going to work on this year, next year, and so on. As the years roll on, you will want to refer to specific chapters that address current problems or concerns. It will then become a guide to you as you grow and develop from boy to man. Make a list of the things you will do to accomplish this year's goals. Then set a date by which you will accomplish each goal. When you have your plans set, talk them over with your parents. Ask them to help you achieve your goals. It would be a good idea to reread this book every year. You may want to adjust your goals or perhaps add new ones. During your time as a priest, obtain a copy of *"Preach My Gospel": A Guide to Missionary Service.* Read and study it as your mission approaches.

Don't try to do everything in one year. If you begin at twelve, you have six years to make the transition from deacon to man of God. Just choose a few things each year and make them a part of your life. By the time you are nineteen, you will be doing great for a young man your age in honoring your priesthood. Heavenly Father will be pleased with you. You will have the Holy Ghost to guide you.

As you read and study this book, you will realize that you are learning and growing in many ways that make life interesting, fun, and adventuresome. You will begin to understand how important your family is to you. You will be doing things you enjoy doing. You will be developing into an adult. You will be a worthy young man. You will be a happy young man. You will be a man of God!

Acknowledgments

To the people who contributed to the preparation of this book, I express my sincere appreciation. I express appreciation to my wife, Ruth, for her support. She has spent many hours reviewing parts of the manuscript and making corrections and suggestions. Thank you, sweetheart, for your help.

I express appreciation to Soren Cox, a neighbor, for his suggestions and corrections. He is a retired Brigham Young University English professor. He has also been a mission president, Missionary Training Center branch president, and MTC district president.

I express special appreciation to Brad Harris, faculty member of the Department of Recreation Management and Youth Leadership at Brigham Young University, who helped with the scouting chapter.

I express appreciation to two of my children: Kumen, my only son, and Cheryl Ann, my youngest of four daughters, whose help with my computer assisted greatly in the preparation of the book.

To Duane Crowther of Horizon Publishers, whose suggestions, encouragement, and guidance have been helpful and used, I express sincere thanks.

I also express appreciation to Michael Morris and Mindy Higginson at Cedar Fort for their help in editing and preparing the manuscript for publication.

Remembering Your Spirit Life with Heavenly Father

Since you were a small boy, you can probably remember singing at home, in Primary, and elsewhere the song, "I Am a Child of God." You learned that Heavenly Father is the father of your spirit. You were born as a spirit into a heavenly family. There you grew as a baby spirit, to a boy spirit, to an adult spirit. You learned that every human being is a child of God. You learned that Heavenly Father loves all of his children regardless of the color of their skin, where they live, the amount of money they have, or their health. Heavenly Father was the father of the spirit of each of his children who later became human beings when they were born into this life and received a physical body. He doesn't like some of the things his children do, but he still loves every one of his spirit children.

"The Living Christ: The Testimony of the Apostles" tells us that Jesus, like each of us, is one of Heavenly Father's spirit children. He was Heavenly Father's first spirit child.

Jesus is the only individual who had Heavenly Father as the father of his physical body as well as his spirit body (*Ensign*, April 2000, 2). That is why we say, "Jesus Christ is the only begotten of the Father in the flesh." "The Family—A Proclamation to the World" states:

> All human beings—male and female—are created in the image of God. Each is a beloved spirit son or daughter of heavenly parents, and, as such, each has a divine nature and destiny. Gender is an essential characteristic of individual premortal, mortal, and eternal identity and purpose.
>
> In the premortal realm, spirit sons and daughters knew and worshiped God as their Eternal Father and accepted His plan by which His children could obtain a physical body and gain earthly experiences to progress toward perfection and ultimately realize his or her divine destiny as an heir of eternal life. (*Ensign*, November 1995, 102)

I hope every young man who reads this book will realize in his heart that he truly is a spirit son of Heavenly Father and was born spiritually of heavenly parents. Heavenly Father knows you better than you know yourself. He has loved you, taught you, and guided you since your spiritual birth so long ago. I like to think that as a spirit boy, spirit young man, and spirit adult you lived with and learned from Heavenly Father. As He taught you, you listened, you learned, you obeyed, you performed, you grew, you progressed toward becoming more and more like Heavenly Father. You were happy, and He was happy with your spiritual progress and growth toward spiritual adulthood. All of this spiritual growth and development did not happen in a relatively short period of time from babyhood to adulthood as it does in this mortal life. It probably happened over an aeon of time.

You were one of billions of Heavenly Father's children, but He knows each one of us individually, and He loves us all. As spirit sons and daughters, we grew and developed spiritually until that development reached the point where if we were to continue to become more and more like Heavenly Father, we had to have other experiences, other teachings, other growth and development we could not obtain as spirits. One of the things we had to obtain to become more like Heavenly Father was a physical body of flesh and bones. We could not get a physical body in our premortal life. Heavenly Father presented a plan whereby we would come to this earth. Our spirit would enter the body of a physical baby and give it life. That body would be an earthly body for our spirit. That would allow us to progress toward becoming more like Heavenly Father, who has a physical body of flesh and bones (D&C 130:22).

A second thing we had to do to become more like Heavenly Father was to learn how to properly use agency—to individually make the choice to do the right thing, the correct thing in any situation. We would be free to choose to do the right thing or the wrong thing. Sometimes the choice we would have to make would be between two or more good things. The choice would be up to us. As we did this in mortality, we would become more like Heavenly Father, who always makes correct choices and always does the right things. He is perfect. We are working and striving to become perfect.

Another thing we had to do to become more like Heavenly Father was to be tested in our physical bodies to see if we would live the way we had as spirits. Heavenly Father knew what we would do when we were with Him. We had done it so well for so long. He had to find out what we would do with all that spiritual growth and development when we were in our physical bodies and not in his presence.

Part of Heavenly Father's plan for our mortal existence is that the memory of our premortal life be hidden from our mortal memory. If we could remember in mortal life all we knew, experienced, and learned in the premortal existence, most of us would probably automatically do the right things without gaining strength of character by doing them for the right reasons and exercising mature use of agency. We would not progress toward becoming perfect individuals like Heavenly Father.

There are many experiences we need to have in this life as we continue to grow, develop, and become more like Heavenly Father that we could not experience as spirits. Among them are being baptized and confirmed, receiving and using the priesthood, making and keeping covenants, beginning an eternal family, loving as Heavenly Father loves, and serving others as Heavenly Father serves.

Another area of challenge and experience in mortality is for us to discover and learn which strengths, abilities, and talents we developed in the premortal life as spirits and brought with us into mortality. As we realize that we do have strengths, abilities, and talents, we will want to continue to improve and strengthen them. We can develop and work on new ones. We will want to use them to bless our own lives and the lives of everyone with whom we come in contact. We will find happiness and joy as we do.

For example, have you known someone who seems to have a talent for music? It seems so natural to them, so easy that they often cannot get enough of it; they seem to do whatever they want to with music. They may have developed this talent to a high degree in the premortal life.

The same thing could be said for an endless list of strengths, abilities, talents, and even gifts. A few of these are:

Being artistic	Building
Teaching	Speaking
Writing	Learning languages
Working	Being a leader
Loving	Being obedient
Being humble	Being family oriented
Being social	Having spiritual skills
Thinking	Being teachable
Being honest	Being service oriented
Being assertive	Being alert
Having a sense of humor	Being trustworthy
Trusting	Being loyal
Making friends	Being kind
Being upbeat	Having a good memory
Forgiving	Understanding
Being sincere	Being genuine
Achieving	Smiling
Being happy	Counseling
Being inquisitive	Being respectful
Being thankful	

Heavenly Father does not leave us alone. He is ready to help us when we ask him. He expects us to use our agency wisely. He won't make us do the things we need to in order to become more like Him. He allows us to use our agency.

He has said, "For behold, this is my work and my glory—to bring to pass the immortality and eternal life of man" (Moses 1:39). He is talking to you. Do your part in helping Heavenly Father bring to pass your immortality and eternal life.

2

Our Family on Earth

Heavenly Father's plan of happiness for His spirit children includes each one being born into a family on this earth with a mother and father to care for, teach, and guide the individual through babyhood, boyhood (or girlhood) and adolescence until adulthood. For most individuals, this is the first eighteen years of mortal life on this earth. As a young man between twelve and eighteen years old, you are well established in your family on earth and over halfway through living at home. You need to learn all you can from your mother and father during the remaining years at home. There are many things they need and want to teach you. Be a good son—listen to your parents, learn from them, obey them, perform as they desire you to perform. It will make life a lot easier and happier when you are on your own.

Most parents still feel they don't have all the answers and are still learning. What really counts is that your parents love you. Your parents want only the best for you. They will do everything they can to provide for your needs in all areas—even before they provide for their own personal needs. For this you should be grateful and thank them often. It is a young man's duty to take advantage of his parent's efforts, pay attention to what they say and what they ask him to do, and obey and honor them.

During your teenage years, your parents will be doing all they can to teach and train you to take care of yourself—to discipline yourself without them having to tell you to do everything as they did when you were younger. The sooner you learn to care for yourself on your own in the ways your parents expect you to will determine how fast you grow up. If you learn to take care of yourself and work consistently within the boundaries set by your parents when you are twelve, thirteen, or fourteen, you will have the advantage over older young men who haven't learned those things yet. As a member of your family on earth, your parents will expect you to become more helpful as a family member during your early teen years. If you have younger siblings, your parents will expect you to take more responsibility for the care of younger children, not just babysitting, but in all their needs, so by the time they are your age, they will be able to care for themselves.

There are probably other children in the family who are older than you. It is so important that you have a loving, working relationship with each of them. As you are finding out, they too are learning to take care of themselves; some may have learned when they were your age; others may be slower and still need to take directions from your parents. However, they do not need instruction from a younger brother. They won't like you reminding them what they should do any more than you like the children younger than you reminding you what you should do.

Families are meant to help each other. Every member

of the family should be concerned about, love, and support every other member of the family. This includes the times they don't agree with what the others may say or do. As you do your part to be supportive, it will make for a happy family life. That's the way Heavenly Father wants it to be.

The hub and highlight of family life is family home evening each week, when the entire evening is devoted to being family night. Family home evening usually begins after dinner and is a formal meeting under the direction of father. By previous assignment, everything is made ready for this important time together. One member of the family will give a lesson, perhaps one prepared from the family home evening manual.

After the lesson often a family council (business meeting) is held under father's direction. This is an opportunity once a week for family members to talk about anything they want to with the family. There will be times that some or most won't have anything they want to talk about. That's all right. They know when they do, they can bring up anything. It's also a good time to bring everyone up to date on the highlights of what has happened in each family member's life the past week and plans and schedules for the coming week. This part of the family council gives everyone an opportunity to bring the family up to date on what's happening to them and what will happen the coming week. Usually the formal family home evening (lesson and family council) will last about an hour, depending on the ages of family members. After the formal family home evening, most families enjoy a family activity, concluding with a treat.

I hope these ideas are not new and have been practiced in your home. However, if you are a young man who hasn't had or doesn't have family home evening regularly, I'd like to suggest a personal challenge to you. Ask your father if you can talk with him alone. When the two of you are alone, say to your father, "Dad, could we have family home evening each Monday evening?" If your father understands family home evening but the family for whatever reason just hasn't been doing it, he may want time to think about it. That is all right. He now knows you, a son he loves, would like to have family home evening and that it is important to you for the family to be together each Monday evening.

If your father does not understand family home evening, perhaps you can ask him to read this chapter in your book and then tell him you would like the family to have family home evening each Monday. Perhaps there is another father in the ward your dad could talk to about how they do family home evening in their home. He may want to talk with the home teachers at a time they are not visiting the family. He may even want to talk with the bishop about it.

In addition to Monday family home evening, there will be many times during the year when the family will have fun activities together. These activity times can be planned during the family council part of Monday family home evening. Fun activities won't happen every week, maybe not even every month, but they are important for the family to have. Your family may enjoy different types of activities than another family. Your family should consider and select fun activities that family members enjoy. The family planning (over weeks or months) and anticipation of the big event most usually is just as important as the activity itself.

If you are a young man who hasn't had or doesn't have family activities regularly, I'd like to suggest a personal challenge to you. Ask your father if you can talk with him alone. When the two of you are alone, say to your father, "Dad, could we plan some special family activities?" He will probably want to know what you have in mind, so have several suggestions ready for him to think about. He will probably want some time to think about it and talk it over with your mother.

I am sure your father wants to use the priesthood he holds to bless his family whenever he can. One way he can do this is to regularly have a father's interview with you and each child in the family. A father's interview is when just you and your dad are alone. You can review any previous plans you have made together of things you will do. You can make new plans for things you need to do. You can talk over with your dad any concerns or things that bother you. You can talk about things that don't seem to be going well for you. You can ask him about things you don't understand (how to repent, how to listen to the Holy Ghost, and so forth). You can ask him about new feelings you are having. You can ask him anything you want to know. The important thing is that you and your dad are open and honest with each other. You should feel comfortable that what you and your dad talk about is between the two of you. It is just as much your responsibility as it is your dad's to keep these father's interviews private and special. It could be a good time for your dad to help you with your Boy Scout requirements or when older your Varsity Scout or Venture requirements.

Many fathers have a father's interview with each child in the family monthly. Some do it every other month, others each three months. You and your dad decide when the regular scheduled interviews will be. The thing you must remember is, as a son, you can request a father's interview any time you want one. You do not have to wait for the regularly scheduled interview. If you want one monthly, ask your dad for one monthly. If you want one now—today—ask him. Most fathers will interview their children individually whenever the child would like. Dad may not be able to give the interview at the time you ask. It will have to be when it is a good time for both of you.

It may be that you are a young man in a home without a father or with a father who does not hold the priesthood. All fathers, whether they are members or not, whether they hold the priesthood or not, can have fathers' interviews with their children. I believe every father should have that kind of a relationship with each child regularly. If your father, regardless of his church standing, has not been having a father's interview with you, go to him and ask him if he would have a father's interview with you. Let him read this chapter of your book, and he will understand what you are talking about.

Never forget, your father loves you, as he does the other children in the family and your mother. He wants you to be healthy and happy. He wants to help you grow into a fine, honorable young man and adult. Take advantage of that help often.

Many fathers will want to end the father's interview with a father's blessing. These often are very special, sacred, spiritual experiences for both you and your dad—the kind you cherish in your heart and don't talk about much with others. There are other times your father may give you a father's blessing other than at the end of a father's interview. This usually occurs on special occasions, such as when you start a new school year, go on a mission, get married, or enter military service. A family may record a father's blessing for family records, but it is not preserved in Church records.

3

Values Are What I Am

You began to set your basic values in this mortal life before you started school. Setting values usually begins at your mother's knee with her help. Father gets in the picture too. At first you didn't understand the difference between right and wrong and probably kept asking "Why?" to everything they said or asked you to do.

Gradually you began to understand what was right, acceptable, proper, and good. You began to say your prayers each night before bed with mother's help; you began to say the blessing on the food before meals; you began to take your turn at family prayer and family home evenings.

Without realizing it, you began to set your basic values—things that would guide you in doing what Heavenly Father and Jesus want you to do. Little by little, these basic values have been added to. Now that you are a teenager, the list of values continues to get longer, and each value stronger as you grow to manhood and continue in preparation to serve your mission, marry in the temple, and become a worthy husband and father.

You will want to be sure that you have the proper set of basic values that Heavenly Father wants you to have. Once a year or so, you should review your basic values with your parents. Such discussions would be appropriate for one of your regular father's interviews. Listen carefully to what your parents tell you in regard to basic values.

Your basic values become the core of your personal strengths. They form your character. They are your ideals, your attitudes, your habits, your purposes in life. They are you. You want them to be the best, the highest possible.

If per chance all this is new to you and you have not made a list of your basic values, please do so soon. It will give direction to your life. Your list of values is your code for living.

Once you have made a list of your basic values, take a good look at it. Study it. Think about it. Then ask yourself, "Are there other values, ideals, attitudes, or habits I want to have but don't now?" List them. Then ask your parents to help you develop a plan for acquiring these new values you desire.

The following is not a complete list of values a young man might have, but it is a good place to start. Continue to add to your list each year as you get older. Some basic values would include:

Prepared	Friendly
Physical strength	Brave
Good manners	Respectful
Caring	Happy
Responsible	Cheerful
Helpful	Reverent
Clean body	Honest

Sense of humor	Clean clothes
Kind	Serving
Clean talk	Loving
Sincere	Courteous
Loyal	Thankful
Dependable	Mentally awake
Thrifty	Morally straight
Trustworthy	Worker
Dutiful	Obedient
Forgiving	Prompt

Even though your years of Cub scouting are past, you probably still remember the Cub Scout Promise, the Law of the Pack, and the Cub Scout motto and still live them. They are a part of your value system. You made them a part of your life when you joined the Cub Scouts, and you have lived them daily ever since.

When you became a Boy Scout, you added the scout oath, the scout law, the scout slogan, and the scout motto to your value list. I hope you are making them a guiding force in your daily life.

As scoutmaster of a National Boy Scout Jamboree troop, I found that in our jamboree troop we had thirty-five scouts and five adult leaders—all members of The Church of Jesus Christ of Latter-day Saints. All thirty-five scouts were active in the Aaronic Priesthood. All five adult leaders were active Melchizedek Priesthood holders.

During a Saturday training session, the newly appointed boy leaders of the troop were encouraged to develop a troop vision statement. I was pleased when they came up with the following troop vision statement, which they presented to the entire troop. It was adopted and memorized; it became what every member strived to live.

Jamboree Troop 2055 Vision Statement:

Troop 2055 is made up of some of the finest young men of the Utah National Parks Council.

We're happy when we're in the right place at the right time doing the right thing with the right people in the right attitude.

We seek opportunities to help our fellow scouts and communities we visit.

We stand as witnesses of God at all times and all places and will honor our priesthood.

Definitions of Some Basic Values:

Prepared: You are always ready in mind and body to do your duty and to face danger, if necessary, to help others. You need to be prepared for life—to live happily without regret, knowing that you have done your best.

Brave: "A scout can face danger even if he is afraid. He has the courage to stand for what he thinks is right even if others laugh at him or threaten him" (scout law). Defend those who are targets of insults, foul talk, slurs, or jokes.

Caring: You feel interest in or concern about someone or something.

Cheerful: "A scout looks for the bright side of life. He cheerfully does tasks that come his way. He tries to make others happy" (scout law). You dispel gloom or worry and are upbeat and positive.

Clean body: Keep your body fit and clean. Wash your body regularly. It's all right to get dirty if it's the kind of dirt that will wash off with soap and water.

Clean clothes: When appropriate, wear clean clothes. It's all right to get yourself and your clothes dirty, especially work clothes or play clothes. However, when work or play has ended, take a bath or shower, and then change into some clean clothes.

Clean talk: Keep your talk clean. Never use foul language. Avoid swear words, harmful thoughts, profanity, and dirty stories which are weapons that ridicule others and hurt their feelings. The same is true of racial slurs and jokes making fun of ethnic groups or people with physical or mental limitations.

Courteous: "A scout is polite to everyone regardless of age or position. He knows that good manners make it easier for people to get along together" (scout law). Be polite to everyone. Open a door for someone. Rise from your chair when a guest, girl, or lady enters the room. Greet others with a firm, sincere handshake.

Dependable: Do what you said you would do, when you said you would do it, and in the best way you can. You can be counted on to perform, do something, or act in an expected way.

Dutiful: Perform the tasks you owe parents and leaders. Perform the functions that arise from your position.

Forgiving: Use the power within you to overcome anger and feelings of revenge. Allow room for error or weakness in others. Give up resentment.

Friendly: "A scout is a friend to all. He is a brother to other scouts. He seeks to understand others. He respects those with ideas and customs that are different from his own" (scout law).

Good manners: Say "please," "thank you," "pardon me," and "sorry" as appropriate. Respect the feelings and needs of others.

Happy: Be pleasant, glad, and upbeat. Have a smile on your face.

Helpful: "A scout is concerned about other people. He willingly volunteers to help others without expecting payment or reward" (scout law).

Honest: Stick to the facts. Keep yourself free from fraud and deception. Have integrity.

Kind: "A scout understands there is strength in being gentle. He treats others as he wants to be treated. He does not harm or kill anything without reason" (scout law).

Loving: Have unselfish loyalty to and genuine concern for others.

Loyal: "A scout is true to his family, friends, scout leaders, school, nation, and world community" (scout law).

Mentally awake: "Develop your mind. Strive to increase your knowledge, and make the greatest use of your abilities. Be curious about the world around you. Learn all you can both in class and beyond school" (scout oath).

Morally straight: "Be a person of strong character. Guide your life with honesty, purity, and justice. Respect and defend the rights of all people. Your relationships with others should be honest and open. Be clean in your speech and actions, and faithful in your religious beliefs. The values you follow as a scout will help you become virtuous and self-reliant" (scout oath).

Obedient: "A scout follows the rules of his family, school, and troop. He obeys the laws of his community and country. If he thinks these rules and laws are unfair, he tries to have them changed in an orderly manner rather than disobey them" (scout law).

Physically strong: "Take care of your body. Protect it and develop it so that it will serve you well during your mortal lifetime. That means eating nutritious foods and being active to build strength and endurance. It also means avoiding drugs, alcohol, tobacco, and any other practices that can destroy your health" (scout oath).

Prompt: Be where you need to be on time. It is good to develop the habit of being five minutes early.

Respectful: Give someone high or esteemed regards.

Responsible: You can be counted on to perform as

expected. You are able to choose for yourself between right and wrong.

Reverent: Have a profound love and respect for Heavenly Father and Jesus, God's creations, and things that are sacred.

Sense of humor: Express the fun side of things without ever making another human being, something sacred, or serious things the object of your humor.

Service: Do things for others without thought of pay or reward.

Sincere: Be pure, genuine, wholehearted, heartfelt without pretense.

Thankful: Feel gratitude for what you have.

Thrifty: "A scout works to pay his way and to help others. He saves for the future. He protects and conserves natural resources. He carefully uses time and property" (scout law).

Trustworthy: "Tell the truth. Keep promises. People can depend on you" (scout law).

Worker: Exert your strength to do or perform something. Stay at a task until it is accomplished. Do what needs to be done when it needs to be done.

As a Latter-day Saint young man, your values, ideals, attitudes, and purposes in life should also include the following:

Accountability: You should be responsible for the choices you make. You should not blame your circumstances, your parents, family, or your friends if you choose to disobey God's commandments (*For the Strength of Youth,* 1).

Gratitude: The Lord wants you to have a spirit of gratitude in all you do and say. "He who receiveth all things with thankfulness shall be made glorious" (D&C 78:19).

Modesty: Your body is God's sacred creation. Respect it

as a gift from God and do not defile it in any way. Through your dress and appearance, you can show the Lord that you know how precious your body is (*For the Strength of Youth*).

"Know ye not that ye are the temple of God, and that the Spirit of God dwelleth in you? . . . The temple of God is holy, which temple ye are" (1 Corinthians 3:16–17).

Proper Use of Agency: Your Heavenly Father has given you agency, the ability to choose right from wrong and to act for yourself. You have been given the Holy Ghost to help you know good from evil. While you are here on earth, you are being proven to see if you will use your agency to show your love for God by keeping His commandments (*For the Strength of Youth*).

"Wherefore, men . . . are free to choose liberty and eternal life, through the great Mediator of all men, or to choose captivity and death" (2 Nephi 2:27).

Sexual purity: "The sacred powers of procreation are to be employed only between man and woman, lawfully wedded as husband and wife" ("The Family: A Proclamation to the World").

"Physical intimacy between husband and wife is beautiful and sacred. It is ordained of God for the creation of children and for the expression of love between husband and wife. God has commanded that sexual intimacy be reserved for marriage" (*For the Strength of Youth*).

The above definitions come from the sources I have already cited, as well as from *Merriam Webster's Collegiate Dictionary*. They also come from the following handbooks published by the Boy Scouts of America:
- *Cub Scout Wolf Handbook* (2004)
- *Cub Scout Bear Handbook* (2004)
- *Junior Leaders' Handbook* (1991)

- *Webelos Handbook* (2000).

4

Aaronic Priesthood Years

Joseph Smith and Oliver Cowdery received the Aaronic Priesthood at Harmony, Pennsylvania, May 15, 1829, under the hands of an angel, who announced himself as John, the same that is called John the Baptist in the New Testament. The angelic visitant averred that he was acting under the direction of Peter, James, and John, the ancient Apostles who held the keys of the higher priesthood, which was called the Priesthood of Melchizedek. The angel placed his hands on Joseph Smith and Oliver Cowdery and said:

"Upon you my fellow servants, in the name of Messiah I confer the Priesthood of Aaron, which holds the keys of the ministering of angels, and of the gospel of repentance, and of baptism by immersion for the remission of sins; and this shall never be taken again from the earth, until the sons of Levi do offer again an offering unto the Lord in righteousness" (D&C 13:1).

Worthy baptized males may receive the Aaronic Priesthood when they are twelve years old or older. It is one of the most important things to happen to you since you were baptized. You probably looked forward to becoming a deacon so you would be able to pass the sacrament. At twelve years old, it is now your turn.

In the bishop's interview before you were ordained a deacon, he talked to you about important things you should have been doing to be worthy to receive the Aaronic Priesthood. These are things you must do for the rest of your life in order to be worthy to use your priesthood. Among the things the bishop should have talked to you about are:

- Praying regularly in private, and participating in regular family prayer.

- Honoring your parents.

- Speaking and acting honestly.

- Treating all people with kindness and respect.

- Being morally clean.

- Refraining from reading pornographic material, going to pornographic movies, or seeing pornographic material on the internet.

- Paying a full tithing.

- Obeying the Word of Wisdom, including abstaining from tobacco, alcoholic drinks, coffee, and tea.

- Refraining from the use of illegal drugs.

- Refraining from using the name of the Lord in vain, vulgar expressions, and other forms of degrading language.

- Doing your duty in the Church and living in accordance with Church rules and doctrines.

- Fulfilling assignments given you by your quorum presidency.

- Attending priesthood, sacrament, and other church meetings.

If you have been faithful as a deacon and are still a worthy priesthood holder at age fourteen, you will be interviewed by your bishop to become a teacher in the Aaronic Priesthood. A similar pattern is followed as was followed when you became a deacon. Likewise, once ordained a teacher, you begin functioning as a teacher and meeting with the teachers quorum. As a new teacher, you will receive instructions from the teacher's quorum presidency on the performance of your duties to prepare the sacrament, usher for church meetings, do home teaching, care for the poor and needy, care for the meetinghouse, give meaningful service, and so on.

Your two years as a teacher will go fast as you magnify your priesthood through worthiness and faithfulness in carrying out priesthood assignments. Stronger feelings and testimony that you are acting in God's name and with His authority for the salvation of the human family will come into your heart. You are doing His work, and you will receive His pay. Think of it when you return home after home teaching and have a special feeling in your heart. Think of it when you help prepare the sacrament and realize that Jesus himself prepared the sacrament when he lived on the earth. Think of it as you reverently go about your duty of ushering for church meetings and an elderly member whispers, "Thank you," when taken to a seat nearer the front of the chapel.

If you have been faithful as a teacher and are still a worthy priesthood holder at the age of sixteen, you will be interviewed by your bishop to become a priest in the Aaronic Priesthood. Think of how you feel when at sixteen years of age you stand at the side of the bishop as he presents you in sacrament meeting to be ordained a priest. Once you are ordained a priest, you should begin immediately to function in your priesthood duties. Usually it will begin with training from the priest quorum presidency (the bishop is the president of the priest's quorum and will meet with the priest quorum each Sunday in priesthood meeting) on administering the sacrament. You then participate with other priests in administering the sacrament in sacrament meeting. Often you will gain an understanding of what you are supposed to do as a priest by watching the older priests as they perform their priesthood duties.

Your years as a priest are especially important years for you to prepare to receive the Melchizedek Priesthood. Your bishop will give you individual, specific direction in what you should do to be ready and worthy to receive the Melchizedek Priesthood and be ordained to the office of an elder. Heed his counsel and begin your preparation at sixteen. Do not wait until seventeen or eighteen and then anticipate a crash program to be prepared to receive the Melchizedek Priesthood and go on a mission. It should have started when you were ordained a deacon at twelve, but if it hasn't, for your happiness and readiness, begin now.

5

Pray Often to
Heavenly Father

Since being baptized and confirmed a member of The Church of Jesus Christ of Latter-day Saints, prayer has become one of the most important parts of your life. You cannot operate without it. Although you do not talk much about it with other people, you should not be ashamed or embarrassed to admit you pray a lot. You will learn that through prayer a power comes into your life that guides you, quickens your mind, and makes you feel you have help in addition to your own strength and abilities. You won't feel right if you do not communicate with Heavenly Father at least every morning when you crawl out of bed and each night before you crawl into bed.

There are also many times you bow your head during the day and say a silent prayer in your heart. If the situation is such that you can be alone, you find a place, kneel, and talk with Heavenly Father. He is always only a prayer away. You can talk with him at any time, any place. The communication line between you and Heavenly Father is never busy. You only have to activate it. He will always listen. After all, you are one of His spirit sons, and He loves you very much.

Sometimes the situation during the day isn't such that you can find a place to be alone to pray to Heavenly Father. You need only adapt your prayer to the situation. It might be in a classroom at school, where you bow your head and silently pray to Heavenly Father in your mind and heart. It might be when you are walking to the front of a class to do a presentation, and you pray with all your heart asking Heavenly Father's help. These prayers He hears and understands perfectly. It might be when you are in a situation and being pressed to do something, answer something, or perform something and you feel that you need Heavenly Father's help. You might have to say, "I need a few minutes alone to think it over," and depending on the situation, get alone, or bow your head as though you are thinking—and in your mind and heart pray and plead for help from Heavenly Father. He is always there for you, if you let Him.

Most of the time, he will answer your prayers with thoughts and feelings. He will send the Holy Ghost to answer your prayer. The Holy Ghost will plant the thoughts in your mind or feelings in your heart. Prayer and your faith in Christ make the difference. If you are not making prayer a powerful, important, and regular part of your day every day then you are selling yourself short and missing out on so much that could make life easier, smoother, and happier.

I assume you understand prayer and how to pray. Just in case it is not the powerful influence in your daily life that it should be, let's review some of the basics, so you will feel comfortable about praying and know how to pray. You always start your prayer addressing Heavenly Father. Then you thank Heavenly Father for some of the blessings he has given you. With so many blessings, choose a few each time you pray and don't always thank Him for the same things every prayer. He needs to know that you really in your heart appreciate the things He gives you. He needs to know you are thinking deeply, sincerely about what you say in each prayer. So speak from your heart, not just your head. The third thing you say in a prayer is to ask Him for specific blessings. It is important that we add to all of our requests, "Thy will be done, Father." We really don't want anything that Heavenly Father knows would not be good for us or is against His will.

The last thing we do is to close the prayer, "In the name of Jesus Christ, Amen." Each prayer we offer should have the same format even though what we thank Heavenly Father for and what we ask Him for would be different if it is a personal prayer, a family prayer, or a prayer opening or closing a meeting. Prayers will also be different from day to day, from prayer to prayer.

As a young man, you should always talk to Heavenly Father in prayer as you wake up and get out of bed in the morning and as you prepare for bed at night. On these occasions, it is most appropriate for you to kneel by your bed as you pray. This would be true wherever you are: in your own room, on a camping trip, on an athletic trip, on vacation—anywhere.

Heavenly Father will answer your every prayer. It may be with a "yes," giving what you ask. It may be with a "no," not giving you what you ask. It may be by giving it to you later. He knows what is best for you. Remember, He hears and answers your every prayer.

When you pray, there is no one between you and Heavenly Father. There are just the two of you if it is a personal, private prayer. If you have developed the pattern of saying in each prayer "Thy will be done, Father," not only are you assuring that the answer to your prayer will be the correct and best one, but you also must be willing to accept Heavenly Father's answer.

One of the things you need to learn about prayer when you are a young man is that a prayer should not just be from you to Heavenly Father. During the prayer, you need to pause and listen with your mind and heart to the messages Heavenly Father sends back to you. By listening during prayer, the two of you can communicate much easier than you trying to listen to Him during all the hustle and bustle.

For example, if you discuss a particular problem or challenge you have during your morning or evening prayer and then pause during the prayer to listen to Heavenly Father, you will know from strong thoughts in your mind or warm, special feelings in your heart what the answer is and what you need to do and when. Try it every time you say your personal morning and night prayer. As you get older, you will understand so much better than other young men your age who don't do so, that Heavenly Father is always there for you.

The Book of Mormon emphasizes the importance of us praying to Heavenly Father with all our mind and heart. It calls praying with all our mind and heart "real intent." For example, in Moroni 7: 6 it says, "For behold, God hath said a man being evil cannot do that which is good; for if he offereth a gift, or prayeth unto God, except he shall do it with real intent it profiteth him nothing." Then a few verses later in Moroni 7:9 we read, "And likewise also is it counted evil unto a man, if he shall pray and not with real intent of heart; yea, and it profiteth him nothing, for God receiveth none such."

Alma gives good instruction to his son Helaman regarding prayer which would be good instruction for every young man today. It is recorded in Alma 37:35–37.

> O, remember, my son, and learn wisdom in thy youth; yea, learn in thy youth to keep the commandments of God.
>
> Yea, and cry unto God for all thy support; yea, let all thy doings be unto the Lord, and whithersoever thou goest let it be in the Lord; yea, let all thy thoughts be directed unto the Lord; yea, let the affections of thy heart be placed upon the Lord forever.
>
> Counsel with the Lord in all thy doings, and he will direct thee for good; yea, when thou liest down at night lie down unto the Lord, that he may watch over you in your sleep; and when thou risest in the morning let thy heart be full of thanks unto God; and if ye do these things, ye shall be lifted up at the last day.

By the time you are a teenager, there is another aspect of prayer you are old enough and mature enough to understand and practice. I am talking about fasting and prayer. As members of The Church of Jesus Christ of Latter-day Saints, we are instructed to fast and pray at least monthly. Usually it is the first Sunday of the month. Many members of the Church begin their fasting with dinner on the Saturday before the first Sunday of each month, skipping two meals. Sunday breakfast and lunch would not be eaten, nor would there be any drinking of water or other drink while fasting. Each member of the Church who fasts should begin each fast with an individual prayer outlining the reasons for fasting.

Each time you fast, reasons or requests will be different. Usually there are several key issues one would be fasting for and praying to Heavenly Father to receive. Then during the twenty-four-hour fast, you should return to your knees often and plead with Heavenly Father for the petitions of the fast. At the end of the fast, you should pray again before breaking the fast. Like any prayer we say, there never is an end to the list of requests we could make of Heavenly Father. However, in a period of fasting and prayer, we select a few key issues and then we plead with Heavenly Father during the fast for these things. Remember, each prayer, even when fasting, should include, "Thy will be done, Father."

The following is only a start. It is not a complete list of things a young man might select to fast for during a specific fast.

- For a family member, friend, or ward member to be made well.

- For help on an important, key exam at school.

- For an understanding of the concepts in a school class.

- For strength to keep yourself morally clean.

- For safety and help to do your best during a high school athletic event. (Not that the team will win, but that members on the team will play their best.)

- For a testimony.

- For forgiveness for sin.

- For the companionship of the Holy Ghost.

There may be times when you will need to fast and pray several times before you receive that for which you are fasting and praying. If what you are praying for is God's will, and you demonstrate sufficient faith while fasting and praying and are trying to live worthy, Heavenly Father will grant you everything for which you fast and pray. I have said many times to young people, "I don't believe we can get Heavenly Father's attention any faster than by fasting and praying. First, He knows we really don't like to go without food and drink for twenty-four hours. Second, He figures that if we really are willing to go without food and drink for twenty-four hours and fast for specific things with sincerity and faith, we must be pretty serious about what we are fasting for." The Brethren have counseled missionaries to fast and pray often but not for more than twenty-four hours at a time because missionaries need their health and strength to carry forth their efforts. A twenty-four-hour period of fasting and praying is sufficient to accomplish its purposes. The same advice would be good for anyone who fasts, even teenagers.

6

Listening to and Following the Spirit

Following your baptism, you were confirmed a member of The Church of Jesus Christ of Latter-day Saints and received the gift of the Holy Ghost. The gift of the Holy Ghost is one of the most important gifts you will ever receive in mortality. It gives you the companionship of the Holy Ghost, a member of the Godhead, when you are worthy. It is a help and a companion you can have the rest of your life by maintaining personal worthiness. The Holy Ghost can help you in many ways. In this chapter, we will talk about understanding the Holy Ghost and listening to him. You will want to read and reread this chapter regularly as you grow to manhood, so you can enjoy this special help Heavenly Father has provided you to guide you back to Him.

The key to taking advantage of the gift of the Holy Ghost is personal worthiness. As you were baptized, your sins were washed away, and you came out of the waters of baptism clean and pure before your Heavenly Father. The challenge in every young man's life is to keep himself clean and pure so he is worthy of the Holy Ghost as a companion. If during the years since your baptism, you have sinned and not repented, you will want to repent so you can enjoy the help and guidance available from the Holy Ghost when you are worthy. You need to make every effort to obey God's commandments. You have been taught what Heavenly Father wants you to do.

Every individual except Jesus Christ sins a lot in mortality. Our challenge as we grow from boyhood to manhood and throughout mortal life is to try our best to not commit sin and eliminate the sins we have by repenting. If we truly repent, we never repeat that sin again. If we truly repent, Christ takes that sin as part of the Atonement; Heavenly Father forgives us, and we no longer have that sin nor need to worry about it. We become worthy of the Holy Ghost in our lives. The Holy Ghost can help a young man like yourself every day of your life, if you will ask and let him. He won't force himself on you, but he is available to help you once you have received the gift of the Holy Ghost.

The Holy Ghost is the messenger of Heavenly Father and Jesus. He is the comforter. He can make you feel good. He can give you peace in your heart, help you feel everything is all right. He can enlighten your mind so you will understand a new or hard subject, topic, or course. But you must be worthy. Never forget that.

Unless you are different from most young men, hardly a day goes by that you are not tempted in many ways. Sometimes by another individual, perhaps even a friend or even a family member who tries to get you to do something, take something not yours, say something that just doesn't seem right to you. If you asked Heavenly Father in your morning prayer to let the Holy Ghost be your companion all day, you will have a feeling in your heart to not yield to temptation.

Your feelings will be that you must not do it, must not take it, should not say it. That feeling is the Holy Ghost trying to help you, trying to guide you. If you obey those feelings, you will be following the prompting of the Spirit.

Let's say you have a hard class at school. Others seem to understand the subject, but you don't. You do your homework. You ask questions in class and try to understand, but it still seems extra hard. If you are worthy and you pray to Heavenly Father to help you understand the class, he will answer your request by sending the Holy Ghost to quicken your mind as you put forth the effort to learn the material. The material will be less confusing and more easily understood. You will understand and learn when you thought you couldn't. You must be humble. You must try your best to learn.

You must thank Heavenly Father for sending the Holy Ghost to help you. In fact, as you learn to recognize the influence of the Holy Ghost in your life, you will constantly want to thank Heavenly Father for that help every night in your personal prayer.

7

Developing a Good Attitude

A friend of mine tells the story of her sister as they were teenagers growing up. The sister was a couple of years older. It seemed to the younger sister that everything the older sister did always turned out great. The younger sister felt that hardly anything she did ever turned out very well. One day she said to her older sister, "How come everything you try, everything you do, always seems to turn out great? Nothing I do ever turns out like it would if you did it. What is your secret?" The older sister said to her younger sister, "It's simple. When I get out of bed each morning, the first thing I put on is a good attitude."

Let us consider some of the aspects of attitude. How can you identify a young man with a good attitude? What about one with a bad attitude? What is your attitude today? What do you want it to be? Perhaps the following comparison will help you begin to get the idea of what it means to put on a good attitude when you get out of bed each morning.

Good attitude	Bad attitude
Upbeat	Indifferent
Positive	Negative
Sees the good in others	Can't see the good in others
Happy	Sad
Optimistic	Pessimistic
Idealistic	Cynical
High achiever	Low achiever
Willing	Stubborn
Faith in self	Lack of confidence
Humble	Self-centered
A doer	Won't try
I can and will	I don't care

It is my experience that young men with good attitudes are liked. People like to be with them. People like them around. Their attitude spreads to others. Young men with good attitudes are successful. They achieve what they work at. They enjoy other people and like to see them achieve too. They don't feel threatened by the success of others. Young men with good attitudes are humble about their abilities, achievements, successes and are quick in private, personal prayer to thank Heavenly Father for His help. They recognize that without Him, they would not have achieved such a high degree of success. They tend to play down public praise because in their hearts they know the source of their achievements and successes. They are not self-centered and prideful.

Think now about your attitude. Overall, do you have a good attitude, bad attitude, or are you sometimes in between?

Developing and maintaining a good attitude is one of your most important and urgent responsibilities as a young man. By applying the above information and suggestions, you will find it easier as the years roll on to be known as one with a good attitude. You will be loved, respected, admired, have friends, and be someone people want to associate with. More important, you will be a happy young man.

Developing and maintaining a good attitude through all your Aaronic Priesthood years will pay great dividends when you go on your mission. Entering the mission field with a good attitude as one of your strengths will endear you to the people in your mission and contribute to you becoming an effective and useful instrument in Heavenly Father's and Jesus' hands.

Developing and maintaining a good attitude after your mission will help you select a wonderful young lady to marry, and it will work wonders in you becoming a good husband and worthy father. It is a character trait that will bless your life and the lives of those around you.

8

Regular Scripture Study

Perhaps when you were baptized you received a complete set of scriptures—the Bible, the Book of Mormon, the Doctrine and Covenants, and the Pearl of Great Price. Or maybe you never had a complete set of scriptures until you were twelve years old. If you don't yet have a complete set of scriptures, spend some of your own money and purchase a set—a really nice set. It will probably accompany you on your mission and be used afterward at school and in your future home.

Now that you have your own complete set of scriptures, use them, read them, study them, ponder them, and pray about them. As you do, you will gain even hidden knowledge. I hope your scripture study has included one or more of the following:

1. Family scripture study
2. Personal scripture study

3. Seminary scripture study (if you take seminary)

4. Scripture study in Sunday School class

5. Scripture study for preparing a church talk

Let's talk briefly about each of these scripture-study routines.

Family Scripture Study

Many young men are fortunate enough to grow up in a family where daily family scripture study is as much a part of the daily routine as breakfast, family prayers, and dinner. In these homes, a regular time is agreed on for family scripture study. Most families find that the morning, before everyone leaves for school or work, is the best time. By agreeing on a morning time, all family members commit to being out of bed at least fifteen-minutes before the agreed time. Those who want to can get up earlier and do those things they need to, such as showering or making their bed. The problem families seem to have with an evening time is some family members have places to go and things to do. If families set a late-evening time, younger children might stay up later than they should, and family members might be tired and not as alert as they are in the mornings.

Whatever time you choose, the important thing is that the family should set and follow a regular scripture study program. Each family scripture study session should begin with a prayer asking for the Spirit to be present to help all family members understand the scriptures studied.

If family scripture study isn't happening in your home now, as an Aaronic Priesthood member, you can make a difference. Suggest to your parents that your family should find a time to study the scriptures together every day. If they agree, you can talk with other children about the idea.

If you are the only member of The Church of Jesus Christ

of Latter-day Saints in the family, your family will probably choose to focus on the Bible. If everyone is a member of the Church, there should be no objection to rotating between the four standard works.

You can have family scripture study any way your family desires. Many families find it works best if family members take turns reading a predetermined number of scriptures. Then it is the next family member's turn. This way, everyone stays involved.

In many families, after each person has read their verses, there is a family discussion on points anyone has a question on or wants the family to discuss.

Much good will come from your family having a regular scripture study program. Love and harmony will grow, family unity will surge, and knowledge of the gospel of Jesus Christ will improve.

Personal Scripture Study

Even with family scripture study, each member of the family is free to study the scriptures as much as desired. For a young man, I believe it would be appropriate and beneficial to select one of the four standard works, and then read five pages in that book each day. It will probably take fifteen to twenty minutes. If you will follow that suggestion, you will be able to read the standard works twice by the time you turn nineteen.

Seminary Scripture Study

When you begin taking seminary, whether it is early morning or released-time, your teacher will challenge you to complete a seminary scripture study program which follows the book you are studying that year. During your seminary years, your seminary scripture study program could be your personal scripture study program, replacing whatever pattern you had previously established and followed. After your seminary years are over, you can choose to continue the seminary scripture study program or return to your own previously followed personal scripture study program.

Scripture Study in Sunday School Class

Most Sunday School teachers for youth classes have established scripture study as the main focus of each week's lesson. Using the scriptures frequently in class, these teachers try to give their students a desire for studying the scriptures, hoping it will become a lifetime experience. More and more, members of the Church are being encouraged to bring their scriptures to church meetings. For you, it would be a good idea to take your scriptures to priesthood meeting, Sunday School, and sacrament meeting. As scriptures are used in the various meetings, find them in your scriptures.

Scripture Study for Preparing a Church Talk

When you are asked to give a talk in priesthood meeting or sacrament meeting, go to the scriptures to begin your preparation. One way to assure the Holy Ghost will be present when the talk is delivered is to read from the scriptures. By using the scriptures, the Holy Ghost comes to bear witness in the hearts of listeners (and the speaker) that the scriptures used are true.

9

Enjoy the Complete Boy Scout Experience

By the time you are twelve years old, you already have completed your first year as a Boy Scout. You are probably a First Class Scout or maybe even a Star Scout now. At least two more years of Boy Scouting awaits you at church while you are twelve and thirteen years of age. Some young men continue their Boy Scout experience until they are fifteen, sixteen, or even seventeen.

When you became a Boy Scout, you voluntarily agreed to memorize and live by the Boy Scout oath, law, motto, and slogan.

Living these codes of conduct is what makes you a Boy Scout. Otherwise you are just a boy in scout uniform attending scout meetings and activities, but you really are not a scout in your heart. Living these codes began when you became a scout and should continue the rest of your life, even after you leave the Scout troop.

In your scout troop experience, your scoutmaster and his

assistants will do their best to make the activities of scouting the way Robert Baden-Powell, founder of scouting, intended them to be. He gave a simple formula for the activities of scouting: "The training of Boy Scouts is done mainly by means of games, practices, and competitions such as interest them." "Games"—for the purpose of picking up elementary knowledge about scoutcraft and for fun; "practices"—on hikes and in camp to master the skills; "competitions" in the form of contests to determine to what extent the skills have been learned and for further practice" (*Scoutmaster's Handbook*). *The Scoutmaster's Handbook,* published by the Boy Scouts of America, has hundreds of scoutcraft games and contests your scoutmaster will suggest as the troop program is planned.

Rank advancements in Boy Scouting are:
- Tenderfoot Scout
- Second Class Scout
- First Class Scout
- Star Scout
- Life Scout
- Eagle Scout

You and your parents should sit down and chart a timetable for your scouting years. Study the various requirements and set a date by which you will earn your ranks and merit badges. Be sure to allow time for service projects, leadership, hikes, and camps. You need time for growing as a scout as you live every day the scout oath, law, motto, slogan. A scoutmaster's conference between you and your scoutmaster will do the same thing, but it is best if you and your parents set some tentative dates first. The scoutmaster has had experience with many other young men, and he will let you know if he thinks your plan is sound and practical.

You should have a plan to earn your Eagle Scout badge,

but all of your focus should not be on the advancement program of scouting. Advancement and becoming an Eagle Scout are important, but they are only one of many aspects of scouting. You should benefit and grow from all scouting has to offer, not just the advancement part.

Other aspects of Boy Scouting that you should have the opportunity to experience, in addition to Boy Scout advancement, include:

- Being an important member of a patrol and making the patrol method work.

- Learning leadership and applying it, beginning in the patrol, then the troop, then perhaps as a member of a council summer camp staff.

- Having a summer Boy Scout camp experience for three or four summers.

- Attending your weekly troop and patrol meetings and mastering the scoutcraft skills taught through games, practices, and competitions.

- Participating in a National Jamboree.

About forty thousand Boy Scouts, along with their adult leaders, have the opportunity every four years to participate in the National Boy Scout Jamboree. The jamboree lasts for ten days. National jamborees of the Boy Scouts of America since 1981 have been held at Fort A.P. Hill, Virginia.

A national Boy Scout jamboree is scouting at its best in all respects. Scouts come from every state of the Union and many foreign countries. Program events are many times more than any scout could possibly participate in if he went night and day the entire time of the jamboree. Big arena shows are massive and spectacular, and they make everyone's spine tingle.

Participation in a national jamboree is a major highlight of a scout's life. Most jamboree participants will never meet more people, make more lasting friendships, see as much of America, and participate in so much scoutcraft as they do during their jamboree experience. Memories will be built that will last forever.

I believe participation in a national jamboree will help prepare you for a mission for many reasons:

- It will give you time (probably longer than you ever have had) to be away from home. You will be responsible for your own decisions and your own behavior without the watchful eye of your parents. You will come to realize what kind of a young man you really are.

- You will learn to appreciate your family more because you will miss them. You will have the years between the jamboree and your mission to appreciate and enjoy them before you move out to serve a mission.

- The effort you put forth to earn your way to the national jamboree will show you what you could and should do after the jamboree to build up your mission savings fund faster.

- The jamboree experience itself will help your ability to adjust to new situations and new people.

As you continue in your progress and become a Varsity Scout, you will gain valuable experience. Things such as service, leadership training, deeper commitment to the Scout oath and law, and association with other scouts will help prepare you for both a mission and life.

When you are sixteen years old, you will be eligible to be a member of a Venturing crew. Venturing helps prepare you for your mission and adult life, getting a job, college, and career. However, leadership development is probably the most important element in Venturing. Venturing offers leadership opportunities to every young man.

Scouting can be one of the most rewarding parts of your life. But remember, you get out what you put in. Participate fully, and you will reap the benefits and be closer to becoming a man of God.

10

Puberty—From Boy to Man

Every boy begins to wonder when he will grow up and become a man. He may wish for it to happen all at once—overnight—but it actually takes a few years. He may wish he could be like older boys—taller, with stronger muscles, a deeper voice, and so forth.

What boys usually don't realize or think about is that all of the physical changes are only one part of puberty. Puberty involves more than growing taller, having strong muscles, and getting hairy, even though these are importance and are visible evidence that puberty is happening to a boy. While all the changes are happening to you physically, mentally, socially, and spiritually, you may wonder, "What is happening to me?" You may have strange feelings physically and socially that you never had before.

In this chapter, I will attempt to address some of these changes that are happening to you. A discussion of the details of what is happening in your body should be a major topic for several father's interviews. As you begin to grow, have strange feelings, or wonder about sexual matters, do not hesitate to discuss them with your dad. He was once a boy like you and experienced all the changes and strange feelings you will experience. If your mother is the family head because there is no father in the home, talk with her. She will be as helpful as she can. She is just as concerned as your dad that you have correct information about the changes that are happening to you during puberty.

If, for whatever reason, you would rather talk with your bishop about your experience of puberty, he will answer all of your questions. Grandfathers and other priesthood leaders are also good sources of information. Talking about puberty with other boys often confuses you because they don't know the answers, they may not have experienced what you have yet, and they don't see the total picture. They are in the process of puberty themselves, and their bodies' growth clock may be different from yours, even though you are the same age. You always have Heavenly Father to talk to and guide you. Remember, he is only a prayer away, and the line between you and him is never busy.

Let's get back to the physical changes of puberty. As young men go through puberty, their genital organs develop, they get taller, their shoulders get wider, their bodies become more muscular, their voice deepens, and they begin to grow hair on their underarms, faces, chests, arms, legs, and genitals.

All of the other changes that happen to you during puberty are caused mainly by the function of the sex glands, or testicles. They produce fluids that have a great effect on your development physically and socially. All of these changes and male body functions are good and are part of how Heavenly Father made our bodies to develop and function. There is no sin in any part of our development.

As your body experiences sexual changes, you will probably become sexually aroused for no reason at all. You may need to hide it from anyone looking at you. Usually a magazine, book, or jacket held in front of you will solve the problem.

Becoming sexually aroused for no reason at all is not a sin. However, if you allow yourself to stay that way for too long, it can lead to sexual sins such as pornography or masturbation. You should find a method of controlling how long you are aroused or how long you let your mind think bad thoughts of any type. I had many experiences with missionaries at the Missionary Training Center who had concerns about these things. I would give them a 3-by-5 card with D&C 4 written on it (it only has seven verses). I would then commit them to carrying the card in their shirt pocket all the time until they had it memorized. Then, whenever they became sexually aroused or had bad thoughts, they would say D&C 4 over and over in their minds or out loud until the bad thoughts or sexual arousal had passed. They later reported that it really worked and helped.

Other priesthood leaders have suggested other methods, including memorizing a favorite Church hymn. I found the song used by most young men with this as their method is "I Am a Child of God." I have known other young men who use something they have memorized such the scout oath and law, the Varsity Scout Pledge, the Gettysburg Address, or a scripture of their own selection.

The important thing is to have a method and then to use it. It will keep you from drifting into any type of sexual sin. A sexual thought may not be a bad sexual thought at first, but usually it will become one soon if you think about it very much. You should get rid of it before it gets to that point. If you will use your method instantly, you can.

Once the sex glands begin working or producing fluids,

they do so night and day the rest of your life. Some of the fluids or hormones produced by your testicles are used by your body to grow and develop. Some your body uses to make you think, feel, and behave like an adult male.

During puberty, your body produces more fluids or hormones than your body uses. The body gets rid of some of the extra fluids during sleep by a nocturnal emission called a wet dream. The sexual stimulation incident to the wet dream sometimes results in strange dream situations. This shouldn't worry you. It happens to almost all young men and is the body's way of emptying the stored up fluids. A wet dream is not a sin. It is the way Heavenly Father created our male bodies to work.

The sexual power Heavenly Father has given all human beings is to be used only in marriage. It gives you the ability to become a father. When you use it any way outside of marriage, it becomes a sin. During your teenage years, even though you are sexually capable of becoming a father, you are not prepared for the responsibility that comes with marriage and having children. You won't be prepared for that important role until after your mission. You must guard the sexual power Heavenly Father entrusted you with and use it only as Heavenly Father wants you to—within the bonds of marriage. If we sin sexually, we will lose the companionship of the Holy Ghost. Any type of sin will distance us from the Holy Ghost, but sexual sin will do it faster and make it harder to regain. Only through repentance can we become clean again and enjoy the Holy Ghost as our companion.

While all these feelings are surging in your body, many other exciting changes are happening to you physically. Your voice box grows so that your voice breaks and after a rather odd-sounding period gets deeper and you sound like an adult man. If you enjoy singing, you find it is a new ball game as your range of notes is much lower than the high range and notes of boyhood. The difficult period with your voice are those times when you begin with the voice of a boy and in the middle of a sentence change to the voice of a man, or vice versa. Every male lives through this period, challenging as it can be.

You grow taller, usually a little at a time, but you may grow up to five inches in one year. Every young man is different; your growth clock is different from other young men. This presents you with many new challenges, including clothes that fit. During these years you need to have the clothes you need but not many extras as you are likely to outgrow them very soon. Another challenge is learning how to use and function in the taller and initially awkward body. Most of these challenges are welcomed and wanted by young men, but you must realize they are challenges and you need to do your part to adjust constantly to the larger body and keep it healthy and strong and functioning without too many tumbles and spills.

One of the important things you can do is to eat healthy food, avoid unhealthy drinks, and get a good breakfast. Strict observance of the Word of Wisdom is a must for every young man if he wants to survive puberty. Get your Doctrine and Covenants out. Now turn to section 89 and read the entire section out loud to yourself.

What more could a teenage young man want in his struggles to become a man than what God promises in verses 18–21? Certainly that promise is real and will happen to him if a young man is obedient with exactness to the Word of Wisdom.

> And all saints who remember to keep and do these sayings, walking in obedience to the commandments, shall receive health in their navel and marrow to their bones; and shall find wisdom and great treasures of knowledge, even hidden treasures; and shall run and not

be weary, and shall walk and not faint. And I, the Lord, give unto them a promise, that the destroying angel shall pass by them, as the children of Israel, and not slay them. Amen.

Modern-day prophets have given further guidelines in *For the Strength of Youth:*

Any form of alcohol is harmful to your body and spirit. Being under the influence of alcohol weakens your judgement and self-control and could lead you to break the law of chastity or other commandments. Drinking can lead to alcoholism, which destroys individuals and families.

Any drug, chemical, or dangerous practice that is used to produce a sensation of "high" can destroy your physical, mental, and spiritual well-being. These include hard drugs, prescription or over-the-counter medications that are abused, and household chemicals.

Never let Satan or others lead you to think that breaking the Word of Wisdom will make you happier or more attractive. (36–37)

Another very important thing you must do during puberty in order to develop properly is to get enough sleep. As you get older, there are more and more things to keep you up at night beyond the time which would allow you the needed eight hours of sleep. Protect your sleep time in order to be a healthy young man.

Another other important thing for you to do during puberty is to have a personal physical exercise program. It may be school gym, sports, or athletic programs geared to your age. If these types of exercise do not seem to meet your needs, talk it over with your dad and mom, and they will give you ideas of what you personally could do at home to maintain a regular personal physical exercise program. They might suggest a personal exercise routine such as jogging, biking, setting up basketball hoops in the yard, or something similar. Because of you, they may think a family exercise program would be beneficial for everyone in the family. Just make sure you give your growing physical body the regular exercise it needs.

There will be other changes to your body during puberty that I have not mentioned yet. One area of change is body hair. You have had some since you began puberty, but as you get older, you may notice more hair on your arms, thighs, and lower legs. As you reach mid-teen to later teen years, you may also start to grow hair on your chest. Some men grow hair on their shoulders, backs, and on the backs of their hands. The increase of body hair does not stop at seventeen or eighteen, when you are considered a fully physically mature male, but continues throughout your life. About the time you begin growing facial hair, you will probably notice hair growing in your armpits. Some young men develop underarm hair before they begin to have facial hair, but for most young men, facial hair and underarm hair appear about the same time. Sometime during puberty you will notice that your underarms perspire (sweat) more, and that your perspiration has a different odor than when you were a boy. Usually eating properly, being healthy, bathing or showering regularly, wearing clean clothes, and wearing deodorant will keep you smelling clean and fresh.

Although it might happen at any age during puberty, most young men get their first facial hair between the ages of fourteen and sixteen. Discuss with your parents when they think you should start shaving. They will probably tell you it is up to you, but you may want to start shaving when you have enough facial hair that people are teasing you about it. As you go through the time from starting to shave until your mission, it would probably be easier if from the start you handled it the way you are expected to on your mission. You are expected to be clean shaven all the time (for most missionaries at nineteen years of age or older, this means every day), no mustache or sideburns.

When all the physical challenges of puberty have been met head on and proper choices have been made, you will emerge as a strong young man, physically confident in your now adult-sized physical body. You will have put off the natural man physically and become a saint. In Mosiah 3:19, King Benjamin told his people: "For the natural man is an enemy to God, and has been since the fall of Adam, and will be, forever and ever, unless he yields to the enticings of the Holy Spirit, and putteth off the natural man and becometh a saint through the atonement of Christ the Lord, and becometh as a child, submissive, meek, humble, patient, full of love, willing to submit to all things which the Lord seeth fit to inflict upon him, even as a child doth submit to his father."

11

Understanding Repentance and Forgiveness

Heavenly Father wants us to learn to make good choices in this mortal life. He has given us our agency, which means the choice is ours. We can do good things and not sin, or we can do bad things and sin. We begin learning right from wrong as a child. By eight years of age, a boy pretty well knows what is right and what is wrong. The challenge throughout life is to consistently make good choices. If you have not settled into a pattern of making correct choices by the time you are a teenager, you need to do so quickly. The older you get, the harder it is to make drastic changes in behavior.

You can make any changes you want anytime in life, but you should not "procrastinate the day of your repentance" (Alma 34:33). Work hard during your teen years on making good, correct choices and avoiding sin. You will be happier when you make good choices. Everyone in this life is constantly struggling to make good, correct choices. When we don't make correct choices, we sin. Every sin we commit is against Heavenly Father's will. Therefore we need to make things right with him. Making things right with Heavenly Father is called repentance.

You need to understand how to repent. Every young man has to repent constantly for one thing or another. Maybe you tell a lie, talk back to your mother, cheat in school, use bad language, look at pornography on the internet, steal, smoke, or masturbate. Each of these things and hundreds of others are sins—they are not the way Heavenly Father wants us to behave. Because you sin regularly, you need to have a regular pattern of repentance.

Because Jesus was the only person to live on this earth who never sinned in his entire mortal life—thirty-three years—he was in a position to do two wonderful things for everyone who has or ever will live on the earth. First, Jesus suffered and atoned (paid the price) for all the sins everyone would ever commit in this life on condition of repentance. Otherwise, Christ's suffering and death for our sins will not have an effect on us, and we will have to suffer as he suffered for our sins. Jesus, during the Atonement, suffered for our sins. He suffered so badly that the Bible tells us he bled from every pore of his body.

So how do you take advantage of repentance? There are several steps.

1. **Recognition.** The first step to repentance is to recognize within yourself that you have done wrong, sinned, broken a divine law, and that the punishment for doing it will occur.

2. **Guilt.** When you realize the seriousness of the sin you have committed, you will feel remorse and guilt. These feelings won't leave you until you repent. The hurt will be there even if you try to hide it.

3. **Forsaking the sin.** You must change with sincerity of heart and make up your mind to never repeat that sin again. Sometimes this step is hard, but you haven't repented until you have given up the sin.

4. **Confession.** Most of the confession (telling someone what you have done wrong) will be to the person you have wronged. You should confess your sins to your Heavenly Father in prayer. You can do this anytime. Your nightly prayer before bed is a good time—then you and Heavenly Father are alone.

   Sometimes you will need to confess sins to your bishop. If you have any question in your mind or heart, talk to your bishop. He will be understanding and will help you and tell you what you need to do to finish repenting of the sin.

   Once you make a confession, you need to ask forgiveness of anyone you have wronged. Any time you sin, you need to ask Heavenly Father for forgiveness. Ask your bishop who else you need to ask forgiveness of if you are not sure.

5. **Restitution.** If possible, you should replace that which was taken or restore that which has been lost. If you steal money, you must give that amount of money back to the person you took it from. Restitution is easily understood when it comes to stealing. You might not understand how to make restitution when it comes to other things: lying, cheating, bad talk, breaking the Word of Wisdom, any type of sexual sin, and disobeying parents. If your sin is one you confess to your bishop, ask him how to make restitution for the sin. For sins you don't need to confess to the bishop, it would be best if you could talk it over with your mother or father and have them suggest what you could do to make restitution for sins that don't seem so obvious as returning money.

6. **Serve and obey God.** The final step of repentance is to serve and obey God. When you constantly ask yourself, "What would Jesus do?" and then try your best to do it, you are serving and obeying God. You need to learn that this part of repentance is most easily done when you do service for other people—beyond those you wronged with your sin. Service to other people, young or old, will bring peace to your heart.

When you feel in your heart that you have done all of the above steps of repentance, you should pray and humbly tell Heavenly Father that you feel you have done your best to repent. Then ask him to forgive you and let you know you are forgiven. Do this every night, sincerely pleading for him to let you know that you have been forgiven. Then listen for an answer. It may come during the prayer. It may come later, when you are not praying. I assure you, it will come if you have done everything you need to in the repentance process and if you plead with Heavenly Father for forgiveness.

Eventually there will come in your heart a definite answer. It might be a warm, peaceful feeling that you seem to feel all over. It might be a strong impression that you have been forgiven. It might be that you don't worry about the sin any more because you have the feeling Heavenly Father has forgiven you. It might come as you think about Heavenly Father and Jesus during the sacrament, listen to a lesson in priesthood or at church, hear a testimony, or bear your own testimony. It might come in a way not listed here. It will come in Heavenly Father's time, not yours. Be assured, it will come.

One missionary had done all the things listed above for repentance and had prayed for several weeks to know whether Heavenly Father had forgiven him. He told me, his MTC branch president:

"I know I have been forgiven. When I got to that point the other night of asking Heavenly Father again with all my heart to let me know I had been forgiven, it was as if Heavenly Father stopped me in the middle of the prayer and said, 'You are forgiven.' I didn't hear a voice. I didn't see anyone. *I felt it!* The feeling was more powerful than if I had heard a voice or seen someone."

When you are on your mission and using the missionary book, *"Preach My Gospel": A Guide to Missionary Service,* you will often refer to Part 3 (Study and Teach), Lesson 3 (The Gospel of Jesus Christ) and what it says on repentance as you prepare to teach investigators.[1]

> The second principle of the gospel is repentance. Our faith in Christ and our love for Him lead us to repent, or to change our thoughts, beliefs, and behaviors that are not in harmony with His will. Repentance includes forming a fresh view of God, ourselves, and the world. When we repent, we feel godly sorrow; then we stop doing things that are wrong and continue doing things that are right. Bringing our lives in line with God's will through repentance is a central purpose of our lives. We can return to live with God the Father only through Christ's mercy, and we receive Christ's mercy only on condition of repentance.
>
> To repent, we recognize our sins and feel remorse, or godly sorrow. We confess our sins to God. We also confess very serious sins to God's authorized Church leaders, who can help us repent. We ask God in prayer to forgive us. We do all we can to correct the problems our actions may have caused; this is called restitution. As we repent, our view of ourselves and the world changes. As we change, we recognize that we are children of God and that we need not continue making the same mistakes over and over. If we sincerely repent, we turn away from our sins and do them no more. We resist any desire to commit sin. Our desire to follow God grows stronger and deeper.
>
> Sincere repentance brings several results. We feel God's forgiveness and His peace in our lives. Our guilt

and sorrow are swept away. We feel the influence of the Spirit in greater abundance. And when we pass from this life, we will be more prepared to live with our Heavenly Father and His Son.

Note

1. Other references include "Confession" and "Repentance" in the Bible Dictionary and *The Miracle of Forgiveness,* by President Spencer W. Kimball.

12

Learning the Joy of Service

When you were a Cub Scout and agreed to live the Cub Scout Promise and the Law of the Pack, I hope you never overlooked nor forgot the last part of the Law of the Pack: "The Cub Scout gives goodwill." You learned as a Cub Scout that goodwill means kindness and cheerfulness. As a Cub Scout, you were always looking for things to do for other people. They didn't have to be big jobs, just little things that helped. By giving goodwill as a Cub Scout you were giving service. Can you remember the wonderful feeling you had inside after you had done something for other people—after you had given service?

As a Boy Scout or Varsity Scout, you have continued your regular pattern of giving service to other people. When you qualify for your Star Scout badge, one of the requirements is, "While a First Class Scout, take part in service projects totaling at least six hours of work. These projects must be approved by your scoutmaster." Likewise, one of the requirements to become a Life Scout is, "While a Star Scout, take part in service projects totaling at least six hours of work. These projects must be approved by your scoutmaster."

The Boy Scouts of America believes strongly that it is important that you give service to other people. That is why these service requirements are part of the higher scouting ranks.

There is a major difference between the service projects for Star Scout and Life Scout and the one you complete for Eagle Scout. With the Star Scout and Life Scout, you can be a follower or a leader. For the Eagle Scout service project, you must be a leader. You must plan, develop, and give leadership to others in a project of help to any religious group, school, or community. When finished, the Eagle Scout service project must be of real value. Your project must be approved by your scoutmaster or Varsity Team coach, your troop committee, and your scout district or council before you begin.

Your Eagle Scout project will take many hours of planning and effort. It does not have to be original, but it certainly can be and will give you great satisfaction if no other scout locally you know of has done a similar project.

In the Book of Mormon, Mosiah 2:17, it says the following on service:

"And behold, I tell you these things that ye may learn wisdom; that ye may learn that when ye are in the service of your fellow beings ye are only in the service of your God."

The *For the Strength of Youth* pamphlet says the following on service:

> Service to others is one of the most important characteristics of a disciple of Jesus Christ. A disciple is willing to bear other people's burdens and to comfort those who need comfort (see Mosiah 18:8–9). Often Heavenly

Father will meet the needs of others through you.

When serving, look to the Savior as your example. Although He came to earth as the Son of God, He humbly served those around Him.

There are many ways to serve others. You can serve in your Church assignments and in your home, school, and community. Seek daily the guidance of the Holy Ghost to know whom to serve and how to help meet their needs. Often the most important service is expressed through simple, everyday acts of kindness.

As you devote yourself to serving others, you will draw closer to Heavenly Father. Your heart will be filled with love. Your capacities will increase, and your life and the lives of those around you will be blessed. (38)

On your mission you will spend two years in the service of your God. You will also spend two years in the service of your fellow men. That is what a mission is all about: serving God by serving your fellow men.

Your entire mission will be spent seeking out the righteous and bearing witness of the restoration of the gospel. You will be an instrument in the hands of Heavenly Father and Jesus in bringing people to Christ. This way you serve Heavenly Father and help him accomplish His purpose of "bring[ing] to pass the immortality and eternal life of man" (Moses 1:39).

13

Social Activities and Social Responsibility

As you grow from boy to man, your friendships will change. In boyhood, having other boys as your friends seemed most important to you. Sometimes you might have felt torn in loyalty between your boy friends and your parents. Sisters and girls in general were interested in different things. You have experienced a shift from having just boy friends to feeling that doing things with girls can be okay. Your relationship with girls will become closer and more meaningful as you get older. Boy friends and young men friends are still very important to you and should be until you go on your mission, but you will find associating with girls more interesting and meaningful to you than you ever thought possible when you were younger.

Church leaders ask you not to date until you are at least sixteen years old. Dating before you are sixteen can lead to immorality; limit the number of other young people you meet; rob you of time needed for school studies, sports, and scouting; cost money you probably do not have; and deprive you of experiences that will help you choose an eternal partner. Hopefully you have obeyed the advice of Church leaders. Even if you are sixteen or older, your social life should include more young women than when you were younger, but you should not be in a hurry to have a single girlfriend that you date exclusively. It would be best for you if that type of a relationship were saved until after your mission. Most young men will get plenty of social life with young women in the normal course of life at school, church, work, and family without worrying about focusing on one or a few young ladies.

During these years of dating before your mission, keep your association with the opposite sex clean, pure, and holy. Church meetings and activities will also provide an increase of social life for you during this period of your life. Sunday School classes, Young Men and Young Women joint activities, and youth conferences all provide the social interaction that is healthy and necessary in your growth and development toward manhood.

It is important that as you enter manhood, you have set in your mind and heart your responsibility to girls and women. A healthy relationship between individuals is supportive and equal. You owe it to the women in your life to always keep their best interests in mind. This begins with your mother and sisters and includes all girls and women you associate with.

Every young man has a social life within his own family. Your family social life includes respecting and honoring your mother. Within an eternal family, your social life with your mother is priceless. Her love for you and yours for her is unique and different from that with any other person. Realize what you have and never do anything to disgrace or sadden your mother. Most young men's social life with his family will include sisters—they may be older, they may be younger. Heavenly Father expects every priesthood holder to treat them with respect. By talking to and observing them in family life, you can learn a lot about girls and young women and how best you can relate to them at school, church, and elsewhere.

In all your social activities, remember the basic principles which will keep your relationships within the bounds Heavenly Father wants them to be as you grow and adjust from boyhood to manhood.

1. Always keep a women's best interests in mind. Never do anything that would not be in their best interests.

2. Always be a gentleman and treat all women with respect.

3. Never hit a girl or woman.

4. Never say anything that isn't uplifting and respectful to a girl or woman.

5. Never touch a girl or woman inappropriately, and never let her touch you inappropriately.

However, there is another aspect to your social life you need to be warned about. You may be singled out by a young woman as being desirable to her. She may try to establish a relationship with you that is unhealthy. She may want you to be her boyfriend and ask you to be hers and no other girl's. She may want to be with you every minute she can. If you do not take control of the situation, you may find other young women keep their distance from you because she has spread the word that the two of you are boyfriend and girlfriend. Don't let this happen.

Just what is dating? Dating occurs when a young man

and a young woman get together for an activity. It could be like going out for dinner, or going to a dance, or going to a play, or going to a concert, or going to an athletic game. It could also be like going on a hike, or going on a picnic, or going to a parade, or going to a movie, or going to a party.

When you begin dating, it is best to go in groups or on double dates. Both you and the young lady will feel more comfortable and awkward situations are less likely to come up. When you are in groups or on double dates, you can learn from each other—what to say, what to do, where to go, how it is important to be home early, how to build trust with parents, how to treat each other with respect, and how to help each other maintain standards. There is safety in numbers. Also, when you are in groups or on double dates, it is usually less expensive because the young men can share transportation expenses. Avoid going on frequent dates with the same young lady. Date a lot of different young ladies, but only those who have high standards and in whose company you can maintain your standards. Make sure your parents meet those you date. Make sure her parents meet you. It is important for you to plan dating activities that are positive and inexpensive and that will help you get to know each other better. Do things that will help you and your date maintain your self-respect and remain close to the Spirit of the Lord.

As I have worked with young people regarding their dating concerns, my advice for protecting each other's honor and virtue is as follows. If either one becomes sexually aroused anytime during the date, he or she simply says to the other, "Time out." Each understands that "time out" means no physical touch of any kind the rest of the date—no holding hands, no hug, no kiss. The next date, physical contact is okay until one or the other starts to become sexually aroused. Then that person would say, "Time out," and there would be no physical touch of any kind the rest of the date.

President Gordon B. Hinckley said, "The Lord has made us attractive one to another for a great purpose. But this very attraction becomes as a powder keg unless it is kept under control. . . . It is for this reason that the Church counsels against early dating" (*For the Strength of Youth,* 24).

At this time in your life, you might not even want to date. This is okay. *For the Strength of Youth* says, "Not all teenagers need to date or even want to date. Many young men and young women do not date during teen years because they are not yet interested or do not have opportunities, or simply want to delay forming serious relationships" (24).

As a deacon, you will likely have little interest in girls, let alone dating. By the time you are a teacher, girls become interesting for most young men. By the time you are a priest, your interest in young ladies will probably become a major preoccupation. The Church says that it is proper and acceptable to begin dating at sixteen. As said earlier, there is nothing wrong with you if you don't desire to date until after your mission.

After your mission, as a man of God thinking seriously about marriage and starting your own family, prayerfully seek Heavenly Father's help in finding your eternal companion. Date many young ladies until you find one you become especially fond of. When you find her and your love for each other develops and you both know it is right, propose to her and start planning your temple marriage. If your dating has been clean, pure, and holy, if you are worthy of each other and have saved yourselves for each other in the bonds of marriage, Heavenly Father will smile on your marriage.

14

Strengthening Your Testimony

During my first four and a half years of service in a branch presidency at the Missionary Training Center in Provo, I had a young elder come to our branch who told me he did not have a testimony.

He said he had lived all his life off the testimony of his parents who were strong, active members of the Church. He had heard his parents bear strong testimony many times both in public and in the family. He said, "They seem so sure about it, I figured it must be true. I believe the Church is true. I believe the Book of Mormon contains the word of God. I believe Joseph Smith was a prophet. I believe Jesus was the Christ, our Redeemer. I believe, but I didn't know for myself."

He continued, "Since coming to the MTC, I realize I must know for myself, or I cannot be a missionary. Will you help me, President, gain my own testimony?"

I had him turn in his copy of the Book of Mormon to

the introduction while I turned to the same page in mine. Then I had him read the last two paragraphs out loud:

> We invite all men everywhere to read the Book of Mormon, to ponder in their hearts the message it contains, and then to ask God, the Eternal Father, in the name of Christ if the book is true. Those who pursue this course and ask in faith will gain a testimony of its truth and divinity by the power of the Holy Ghost.
>
> Those who gain this divine witness from the Holy Spirit will also come to know by the same power that Jesus Christ is the Savior of the world, that Joseph Smith is his revelator and prophet in these last days, and that The Church of Jesus Christ of Latter-day Saints is the Lord's kingdom once again established on the earth, preparatory to the second coming of the Messiah.

I said to this humble elder, "There you have it. That is what you have to do to gain your own testimony. I believe the promise made in the introduction to the Book of Mormon. If you will read in the Book of Mormon at least thirty minutes of day each day of your mission as missionaries are asked to do . . . if you will ponder in your heart the message contained in the Book of Mormon as you read each day, and then if you will pray and ask God, the Eternal Father, in the name of Christ in faith if what you have read and pondered is true, you will gain a divine witness from the Holy Spirit [your own testimony] that it is true. If you will do this every day, somewhere in your reading, pondering, and praying, you will have the Holy Ghost tell you in your heart that it is true. From then on, you will know."

I continued telling this missionary, "When you gain your own personal testimony that the Book of Mormon is true and comes to us from God, you will find that you will also gain three other important testimonies. You will gain a testimony that Jesus Christ is the Savior of the world, that Joseph Smith is his revelator and prophet in these last days, and that The Church of Jesus Christ of Latter-day Saints is the Lord's kingdom once again established on the earth, preparatory to the second coming of the Messiah."

He said to me, "I have read in the Book of Mormon at least thirty minutes every day I've been here, and I still don't know if it is true. I believe it is, but I don't know that it is true."

I inquired, "Have you also pondered and prayed asking in faith each day as you read in the Book of Mormon?"

He replied, "Most of the time."

I said, "Do it all the time."

He said he would.

Week after week, he assured me he was doing everything we had talked about, that he didn't have any unrepentant sin, but the promised witness hadn't come. After five weeks at the MTC in Provo, now three weeks before he was scheduled to leave for his mission in Costa Rica, he began to be frantic.

In one weekly interview, he said, "President Skinner, I can't go tell the people in Costa Rica that the Church is true, that the Book of Mormon is the word of God, that Joseph Smith was a prophet, and that Jesus is the Christ and our Savior when I don't know it myself." I reassured him that he would gain a testimony if he persisted in doing what we had talked about, kept himself worthy, and continued asking Heavenly Father in earnest, humble prayer for a testimony. My reply to him wasn't good enough; he exclaimed, "I've got to know if it's true before I leave the MTC!" We set a time between his second and third week prior to leaving the MTC for a special fast that he would gain a testimony. We both fasted two meals and prayed often, individually. Nothing changed.

By this time he had just about convinced himself that he should go home and not to Costa Rica. He kept assuring me he was doing what we had agreed on every day and had since our first interview on the subject. I kept bearing testimony and assuring him that what the introduction to the Book of Mormon promised would happen.

About a week prior to his scheduled departure to Costa Rica, he said, "President, I am not going to Costa Rica to tell the people that I know the Church is true, I know the Book of Mormon is the word of God, I know Joseph Smith was a prophet, and I know Jesus is the Christ, our Savior when I don't know for sure."

I told him, "Elder, I hope you never, never tell anyone in your whole life that you know something is true when you do not." Nothing I said seemed to change his feelings that he should go home and not to Costa Rica. I begged him to hold on his last week at the MTC. Something surely would change.

One night during his final week at the MTC, I visited the residence hall of the missionaries from our branch. I entered his room to chat with each missionary. As I entered, he was on his bed on the top bunk. He jumped down. I started to give him a hug and ask how he was doing. He stopped me by putting his hands on my shoulders and pushing me away. Then looking into my eyes with tears in his, he said slowly and with heartfelt emotion, "I know that the Book of Mormon is true. I know that God lives. I know that Jesus Christ is the Savior of the world. I know that Joseph Smith is his revelator and prophet in these last days. I know that The Church of Jesus Christ of Latter-day Saints is the Lord's kingdom once again established on the earth, preparatory to the second coming of the Messiah."

We then hugged and both felt the power of his own testimony.

I ask you, as a teenager, do you have a testimony? Do you know that the Book of Mormon is true? Do you know that

God lives? Do you know that Jesus Christ is the Savior of the world? Do you know that Joseph Smith was a prophet? Do you know that The Church of Jesus Christ of Latter-day Saints is the Lord's kingdom once again established on the earth, preparatory to the second coming of the Messiah? If you know these things, you have a testimony. It came to your heart by the power of the Holy Ghost. You have special, strong feelings in your heart each time you bear testimony of these things. You know in your heart they are true even when you are not vocally bearing testimony.

If you only believe, like the elder in my story, but want to know for yourself, you can by doing the very same things he did. You can do it at any age. It is my opinion that you are old enough now to have your own personal testimony if you don't already and that you should not wait until you enter the MTC to struggle to get one.

But getting a testimony is a personal event, a private happening between you and Heavenly Father. If you gain a testimony and keep cultivating it, it will be a powerful force the rest of your mortal life. By living true to your testimony, you will be a very different individual. You will have something sacred and dear to you that most young men your age in the world today do not have.

Remember, the formula for gaining your personal testimony is given in the introduction to the Book of Mormon.

"We invite all men everywhere to read the Book of Mormon, to ponder in their hearts the message it contains, and then to ask God, the Eternal Father, in the name of Christ if the book is true. Those who pursue this course and ask in faith will gain a testimony of its truth and divinity by the power of the Holy Ghost."

You probably will have to work at gaining a personal testimony just like the elder did. It may come quickly; it may take several weeks; it may take several months; it may take several years. How long it takes is entirely up to you. If you will do all of the things outlined in the introduction to the Book of Mormon sincerely with all your heart, it will come quickly. If you go through the motions but not completely, it will take a long time. For example, reading the Book of Mormon alone will not give you the testimony of its truth and divinity by the power of the Holy Ghost. As you read the Book of Mormon you must ponder in your heart the message it contains then ask Heavenly Father in faith in the name of Christ if it is true. When you do it completely, the testimony always comes.

Once you have your personal testimony, you must continually strengthen it. There are many ways to strengthen your testimony. Some of the ways I have seen individuals strengthen their testimony include:

1. Continue to live a worthy life, as free of sin as possible. You will make mistakes—everyone does—but don't let any of them be the big sins. Each week, repent of your sins—those little ones—and determine not to make the same mistake again the coming weeks. A good time is in preparation to partake of the sacrament each week. The sacrament is a good time each week for a general self-inspection to see what you need to do to have the Holy Ghost as your constant companion. His companionship will help you live a worthy life.

2. Maintain a daily scripture study of the Book of Mormon. Take time to ponder the message you studied that day in the Book of Mormon. Then ask Heavenly Father in faith in the name of Christ if it is true. If you sincerely and earnestly do this, you will find your testimony of the Book of Mormon will get stronger and stronger, as will your testimony that God lives, that Jesus Christ is the Savior of the world, that Joseph Smith was a prophet, and that The Church of Jesus Christ of Latter-day Saints is the Lord's

kingdom once again established on the earth, preparatory to the second coming of the Messiah.

3. Bear your testimony. Whether you bear your testimony in your heart, in a testimony meeting, or to an investigator, bearing your testimony will strengthen it.

4. Listen to the testimonies of other people, especially in monthly testimony meeting the first Sunday of each month.

5. Write your testimony. Perhaps you could write it on a sheet to be inserted in the front of a copy of the Book of Mormon missionaries will distribute to people in the mission field. Perhaps on a sheet to be inserted in the front of a copy of the Book of Mormon you give a nonmember friend as a gift. Perhaps as you write your testimony in a letter to a relative or friend.

15

Pride Can Destroy You

One of the elders who was in my branch wrote me a special letter to be included in letters for my retirement from teaching at Brigham Young University in March 1996. He said:

> I regret that I was unable to attend your recognition banquet, so I must settle with writing a few words of gratitude to show my appreciation. I remember as a young and very prideful nineteen-year-old boy, I strolled into the MTC with visions of grandeur thinking that through my power I was to bring thousands of people to God's kingdom.
>
> I guess it was the first or second Sunday that you pulled me into your office to tell me I was called to serve as district leader, but that you and the presidency were very concerned about my pride preventing me from serving righteously.
>
> Nothing up to that point in my life hit me in the face harder than that comment, yet I knew it was from a loving president and friend who was concerned for a boy

and a group of boys he hardly knew. That was only the beginning of what was to become a school for me in love and understanding that you taught through example and feeling.

Each time you would grasp my hands and pierce me in the eyes with your true love for the Lord, His work, and His servants in our interviews, I would be left only with the feeling to return that love.

Then you taught me the principle of repentance, which I know I have mentioned before, and I can never forget. My life has been forever changed by you, and through you the Lord continues to teach me of Him. . . . I guess all I can say is thank you for being you and loving me and helping mold me into the missionary that the Lord wanted and knew I could be."

Love,
Elder —————

A boy begins public education at five or six years of age. By the time he becomes a deacon, he is probably in sixth or seventh grade looking forward to junior high and high school. Hopefully when you reach that age, your parents, Church leaders, and teachers have impressed upon you the importance of getting as much education as possible. Hopefully you have taken this counsel seriously. In order to stick to the goal of obtaining the education that will make you productive as a husband, father, and man of God, you must maintain humility. Otherwise you will develop an attitude of pride. "I can make a good living without more education," or, "University schooling isn't for me; I'm not interested in book learning," or, "If I can't get into a university, I'm not going to a trade school or specialty college." All of these are indications of pride. You might be gifted for a trade school or specialty college. You may have to work hard or take special classes to get into the university where you desire to study. You may have to delay other things such as buying a new car or home or travel until your education is completed. To take any of these actions requires humility. Be ye humble always! Seek Heavenly Father's help in making your decisions and achieving your educational goals.

Prior to about age fourteen, most boys and young men are teachable, meek, submissive, loving, unpretentious, not arrogant or dominating, and easy to get along with. Then, with the onset of puberty, things begin to change—not only physically but also socially, mentally, emotionally, and spiritually. It is a big challenge for every young man to handle all the changes in his life and maintain balance. Most young men at this age struggle with pride. A "my will" attitude seems to take over everything they do. It is easy to develop a know-it-all attitude too. In some, an inordinate and unwholesome amount of self-esteem is displayed. They are less teachable, meek, and submissive. Disdain develops on many levels—especially in the family with the younger brothers and sisters. Disdain may be manifested in the classroom toward those whose grades are not as high, in athletics toward those who are not as good, or in Church toward those who are younger or in a less-visible calling. With pride growing so rapidly, he wants to be the best ball player, the best student, or the most popular guy at school. Often he sees the positive result of these desires in his mind, but no one else does. This upsets him inwardly because in his mind and heart he is a winner, and he can't understand why everyone can't see it and give him the recognition he deserves.

Fortunate and blessed is the young man whose parents taught him to look to Heavenly Father for guidance in his life and to make all his requests of God be, "Thy will be done, Father, not mine." When this attitude is reinforced daily by having the companionship and guidance of the Holy Ghost, this young man never leaves the realm of being humble. If you first say, "Please help me achieve this," "Bless me that . . ." or "Make this happen" before considering the Lord's will, you are becoming prideful rather than humble. I hope you are a well-trained and well-guided young man who often asks, "What would God have me do with my life?" rather than "What do I want out of life?" Follow the example of Jesus in everything you do.

People think of humility and pride in many different ways. Let's take a look at both the worldly and spiritual view of humility and pride and see how in reality they are very much alike.

Webster's dictionary gives the following definitions:

Humble: Not proud or haughty. Not arrogant or assertive. Reflecting, expressing, or offered in a spirit of deference or submission. Unpretentious.

Pride: The state or quality of being proud. Inordinate self-esteem. Conceit. Reasonable or justifiable self-respect. Delight or elation arising from some act, possession, or relationship. Haughty and disdainful.

In a conference talk published in the May 1986 *Ensign* called "Cleansing the Inner Vessel," President Ezra Taft Benson defined humility and pride this way:

The opposite of pride is humbleness, meekness, submissiveness, or teachableness. . . . Humility responds to God's will—to the fear of His judgments and the needs of those around us. (6–7)

Pride is a "my will" rather than "thy will" approach to life. . . . Pride does not look up to God and care about what is right. It looks sideways to man and argues who is right. Pride is manifest in the spirit of contention. . . . Pride is characterized by "What do I want out of life?" rather than by "What would God have me do with my life?" It is self-will as opposed to God's will. . . . Someone has said, "Pride gets no pleasure out of having something, only out of having more of it than the next man." (6–7)

In the scriptures there is no such thing as righteous pride. It is always considered as a sin. We are not speaking of a wholesome view of self-worth, which is best established by a close relationship with God. But we are speaking of pride as the universal sin, as someone has described it. . . .

Was it not through pride that the devil became the devil? Christ wanted to serve. The devil wanted to rule. Christ wanted to bring men to where He was. The devil wanted to be above men.

Christ removed self as the force in His perfect life. It was not *my* will, but *thine* be done. (6)

As you move through your teenage years, you will find that as you mature mentally, you want more independence. You are not a little boy anymore. You can think for yourself. You can make decisions. You don't think you need your parents or anyone else telling you what to do all the time. You believe you understand things perfectly. It becomes hard to understand why your parents and others can't seem to see things the same way as you do.

You probably wish your mom would let you be yourself and stop telling you what to do and when to do it. You are becoming an adult, and you would like directions and suggestions to come more from Dad rather than Mom. It is normal for you to have these thoughts, but don't leave Mom out of your life. You will always need her. She can understand her boy is now a young man and wants more independence. Talk it over with her. She will give you more independence as you demonstrate that you can be responsible with it. You can do this by making good decisions with that independence. When you fail to be responsible, she will need to take away some of your independence until you can prove yourself again.

When you begin having these strong feelings for more independence, talk it over with your dad. Make it a topic for a father's interview. You may be surprised to learn how your dad felt when he was your age. He, like Mom, will give you more independence as you demonstrate you can be responsible with it.

What you need to keep in mind as you move through life is that your parents have made the transition to independence. They have had more experience. They have learned responsibility always accompanies independence. They understand what you are experiencing. Also, your parents can provide you with important things you are probably not ready to provide for yourself. They can continue to give you the security of a family life, food, shelter, clothes, education, and love. You are not yet ready for the responsibility that goes with complete independence for yourself, and you certainly are not ready for the responsibility of providing for anyone else in addition to yourself.

The quest every young man experiences as he struggles and yearns for more independence is really a struggle between humility and pride. It takes humility for a teenage young man to say to his parents, "Thy will be done." Recognizing your limitations will help you maintain that humility as you continue to gain independence.

A second area of mental change is the "I know it all" attitude. As you mature mentally and learn more things at school, at church, in the family, and elsewhere, it is easy to develop the attitude of being a know-it-all. This know-it-all attitude will lead you to feel that parents, brothers and sisters, and a lot of other people don't know anything, or at least not as much as you do. This kind of attitude can make it hard for people to work with you and help you.

We've heard the saying, "A little learning is a dangerous thing." Proverbs 4:7 says, "In all thy getting [learning] get understanding." Perhaps these two statements will help you through puberty. It is all right to know it all, if you really do. If you really do know it all, you won't have to tell anyone or have a know-it-all attitude. People will recognize your knowledge, and if that knowledge is tempered with understanding, they will respect you.

You need to avoid pride in all its forms. You need to remain humble. You do it by learning all you can with the help of the Holy Ghost and acknowledging that everything good comes from Heavenly Father. You should be grateful for your knowledge and understanding of things and people, but don't allow yourself to feel that you are better than anyone because of it.

As we summarize this chapter, remember pride is something you will have to struggle with all your mortal life. If you are teachable, meek, submissive and never develop a know-it-all attitude, then you will be a humble young man now, a humble missionary in a few years, a humble husband and father and Church leader after your mission, and one happy individual throughout your life.

Now back to my missionary friend I told you about at the beginning of this chapter. He turned his life around. He got rid of the pride he had as he entered the Missionary Training Center. It took a while beyond his MTC experience before all the pride was gone.

When he got to the mission field, the refining process continued during his first two or three months. Then, when he was completely humble, Heavenly Father could and did use him as an effective and powerful instrument in His hands. He was a wonderful missionary who enjoyed having the Holy Ghost as the third member of his hard-working companionship.

In a letter he wrote to me after being in his second area only a short time, he said, "We are working hard. We feel the Spirit as we teach the people. The people feel the Spirit, accept the message, and many are baptized. You know,

President, it's not me, it's the Spirit that makes the difference."

16

The Call to Serve

If you think about it, you have been preparing for your mission call all your life. Everything you have done and are still doing is preparing you for your mission. Your school work, your church activity, your family life, your father's interviews, your mission savings, seminary, scouting, Aaronic Priesthood activities, sports, regular scripture study, service projects, and your part-time job all have a major part in your mission preparation—and the list goes on. I hope that you have learned how to pray and do so at least twice a day; how to listen to and follow the Holy Ghost and have him as your constant companion; how to be humble and not prideful; how to maintain clean thoughts, clean habits, and clean talk; how to handle responsibility; how to honor mother and father; and how to acquire your personal testimony.

Life hasn't all been smooth sailing. You have made mistakes. You have sinned and offended Heavenly Father. But you are ever so grateful that you have been taught repentance and know how to repent and have repented all your life. Tough as it was, you are grateful to your loving bishop who has helped you if you had serious problems. You know what it is like to feel the Savior's love when you repent. As you plead sincerely for forgiveness in prayer so often, in your heart came the feeling that you are forgiven.

Although your entire mortal life from birth to mission is really the process to the call to serve, I would like to outline the final process.

At your eighteenth birthday interview, your bishop will likely do a number of things. First, he will make sure that you are worthy and that you meet all the requirements to be a missionary. If he finds you are not fully worthy at eighteen, he will outline specifically what you need to do to repent of all your sins so you will be 100 percent worthy by the time you are nineteen. Second, he will likely go over missionary papers, so you are familiar with mission requirements and procedures.

Your bishop will suggest an appropriate time for you to begin working on your missionary papers. This will usually be a few months prior to your nineteenth birthday. He will also probably have you thinking about an appropriate time for receiving the Melchizedek Priesthood and an appropriate time for you to go to the temple to receive your temple blessings.

Your bishop will schedule your mission interview a few months before you turn nineteen. It will be timed when he feels that you can do all the paperwork related to your mission call, have all the necessary interviews, and have the papers submitted to the Church Missionary Committee timed so you will receive your mission call when you have indicated you will be available (end of a school year, end of a work contract). At this interview, he will do a number of things. First, he will make sure that you are worthy and meet all the requirements to be a missionary. Second, he will give you your missionary papers to fill out. Some of the pages you will complete require a medical exam, dental exam, and a missionary picture. You will need to make an appointment for your medical doctor and dentist to complete those sections of your missionary papers. When you have your missionary picture taken, be sure that you dress in your Sunday best and that your hair is as it should be. Your bishop will instruct you on this. Your bishop will set a time for you to complete your missionary papers and related items and to return them to him. Try to do it by the appointed time or before. He will then outline to you what will happen after he receives your missionary papers so you will know what to expect. He will explain to you that he will submit your papers to the stake president, who will want to interview you in depth to determine your worthiness and preparation to be a missionary.

When the stake president is satisfied, he will send your papers to the Church Missionary Committee. After your papers have been processed, they will be submitted to the prophet, who will issue your call to a specific mission. Then the missionary committee will send you your official mission call, material related to your mission, and the date you are to report to a missionary training center.

I firmly believe and testify that all mission calls come from Heavenly Father through his prophet and is the right mission for the missionary. Heavenly Father knows you better than anyone, and He knows where you can best serve. If you can accept the fact that your mission call came from Heavenly Father and serve with all your might and strength, before the end of your mission, you will understand why Heavenly Father called you to that specific mission. Such was my mission call, printed in this chapter from chapter 15 of my personal history-autobiography volume I.

My Mission Call

I grew up thinking that when I was old enough, I would fill a mission for The Church of Jesus Christ of Latter-day Saints. I had watched many young men from our ward go on missions and listened with great interest to their reports following their missions. I wondered often where I would go and if I would grow in the gospel, confidence, and abilities like all missionaries seemed to do.

As I approached graduation from Gila Junior College with two years of college behind me, I was yet eighteen years old and would turn nineteen on June 26, 1950, a month after graduation. The practice of the Church at the time was that young men would receive calls as they turned twenty years of age. I was a full year younger. This was because I had completed the first and second grades of school in one year. My bishop was Chester A. Peterson, an attorney in Safford, Arizona. Inasmuch as I had completed two years of college, he thought there might be a chance that the Church would let me go at nineteen instead of twenty years of age.

Bishop Peterson got permission of the stake president to submit my mission papers to the brethren in Salt Lake City, so by appointment one day I met with him in the bishop's office, and he completed the papers. He asked me many questions. One of them was, "Is there any place you feel you have to go on your mission?" I said, "No." Another questions was, "Is there any place you will not go on your mission?" I said, "Put down a Spanish-speaking mission, Bishop." He dropped his pen and said, "Do you really want me to put that down?" I knew I had jarred him with my reply. When he said, "Do you really want me to put that down?" I knew I had said the wrong thing.

I thought, searching my soul. I really didn't want to

go on a mission to a Spanish-speaking country. My worst grades in high school had been in Spanish. It had seemed so hard. But my bishop, who was trying to get me on a mission a year earlier than normal, was surprised that I was not willing to go anywhere. Finally, I said to him, "No, Bishop, I suppose if the Lord wants me to go on a Spanish-speaking mission, I will go." He said, "Fine," wrote on the paper that I would go anywhere, and went on to the other questions.

Weeks later when my mission call—dated March 14, 1950, in Salt Lake City, and signed by President George Albert Smith—arrived, I was full of anxiety as to where my call would take me. I got the mail from the mailbox and rushed into the house, announcing to my mother and my sisters that my mission call had arrived—even before opening the letter. After all, it was from the office of The First Presidency of The Church of Jesus Christ of Latter-day Saints.

I had thought during the weeks between my interview with the bishop and my mission call, "Surely I'll go to an English-speaking mission in the states, or to England, or even to a European country where the language would be a lot easier to learn than Spanish." As everyone gathered around waiting for me to open the letter and find out which mission would be my mission, anxiety mounted. I scanned the letter quickly, at first looking only for the place. There it was near the latter part of the letter: "Trusting that you will do your utmost to discharge honorably the responsibility herewith placed upon you, and always strive to be a loyal, devoted servant of the Lord, we now extend to you this official call to labor as a messenger of truth in the Uruguayan Mission."

There it was: Uruguay. I was so relieved it wasn't a Spanish-speaking mission. My mind immediately went to the southeastern part of Europe—Yugoslavia, Romania,

Bulgaria, and so forth. I hurried to find a map of Europe. Then I searched it twice trying to find Uruguay, which I knew surely had to be there. Mother kept saying, "I think you had better look in South America." Finally to please Mother, I got out the map of South America, and there it was—south of Brazil and north of Argentina. It was so small that they had to write the name Uruguay in the Atlantic Ocean. Immediately I wondered what language was spoken—Spanish or, I hoped, perhaps Portuguese. A check revealed Spanish as the official language. My heart sank. "Why would Heavenly Father, knowing how tough Spanish was for me and how I felt about Spanish, call me to a Spanish-speaking country?"

It would be almost two years later—just under a year before the end of my mission to Uruguay—before I would understand why Heavenly Father had called me there and realize that it was the right mission for me and that He had a special work for me to do there.

At the time, all I could think was that I must learn Spanish, but I knew that without a lot of help from Heavenly Father, it would be impossible. My mission, as were all foreign speaking missions then, was for 2½ years instead of the usual two years where English was the spoken language. We spent a week at the Mission Home in Salt Lake City and then went directly to our missions without any language training as missionaries receive today.

My problem with Spanish was even deeper than I knew. I was to have a very difficult time with the language because I am tone deaf musically inasmuch as many sounds I don't hear or differentiate between. When I arrived in Uruguay in July 1950, I felt as if I had been removed from one world and put into another. I felt most uncomfortable. *Surely this must be similar to the differences between the three degrees of glory in the eternities,* I thought.

With me, it was not a matter of being unable to understand Spanish, it was worse. I couldn't even tell where one word stopped and another began.

By the time I reached Uruguay, I had about four months of sincere praying to ask Heavenly Father for an understanding of the language of Spanish—for a gift of tongues. I sincerely believed my Heavenly Father could enlighten my understanding of Spanish so I could speak and understand it. I not only believed He could, I also believed He would—my faith was that strong. After all, He had called me to serve in Uruguay. Why wouldn't he give me a gift of tongues in Spanish? I kept on praying earnestly.

The morning after my arrival in Montevideo, Uruguay, my companion and I began Spanish classes—a practice that happened for about an hour each morning most of my mission. The months came and went, and I marveled how smart the other missionaries were—especially my companions. I began to feel that I never would learn Spanish. My first companion had me say a prayer and one of the sacrament prayers (reading both) my first Sunday in the mission in La Floresta Branch. As I reflect, those good people must have really bitten their tongues during the prayers to not laugh at my pronunciation. I kept trying to learn Spanish. I read regularly alone and with my companion the Book of Mormon, trying to get the hang of the language. It just wouldn't come.

I received a transfer to Paraguay and was the seventh Latter-day Saint missionary to that country, which was part of the Uruguayan Mission. Elder Keith J. Morris of Mesa, Arizona, was my second companion, and spoke Spanish perfectly. He tried to help me during the 4¼ months we were together. By the time I had been in my mission for six months, the natives were thinking, "Here is one who won't learn Spanish."

Oh, how my heart would cry. I wanted to be a good missionary. I wanted to understand the people and be understood. I wanted to learn Spanish. I studied. I prayed. I studied. I prayed. I studied. I prayed for a gift of tongues in Spanish.

It was toward the end of my first year on my mission when it began to happen. The first time I was aware of it happening was one night (like many) when I was giving a talk in sacrament meeting. Only this night was different. I had studied, prepared, and written out my talk as always, but when I stood to give it a special peace and feeling came over me. I gave the talk I had prepared, but instead of stumbling over every word once I began the words just seemed to flow out. What was even more important, the people paid attention more and seemed excited over what I was saying. I had never had that happen to me.

That night in Paraguay when I went to bed I cried unto the Lord thanking my Heavenly Father for answering my prayers and giving me an understanding of Spanish. Now I could build on a gift of tongues.

With my Heavenly Father's help, I did build on it. With lots more hard work, more prayer, more struggling step by step, I learned Spanish. Gradually I got to understand most all the people said, and they began to understand and communicate with me without my companion having to translate or clarify to them. It all began to be a natural process with that sacrament meeting in Paraguay.

A few months after this Paraguayan experience at sacrament meeting, President Lyman S. Shreeve, my new mission president, made me a senior companion, called me back to Uruguay from Paraguay, and put me in charge of scouting in the mission in Uruguay. I had never met the man personally up to that time.

With that responsibility, continued study, and continual

help from Heavenly Father, I was able to learn Spanish and communicate with the Uruguayan people.

Even though my Spanish accent was far from perfect (everyone always knew when I spoke that I was a foreigner), it made a difference to be able to understand and be understood in a foreign tongue.

Upon completion of my mission in March 1953, I returned home and on to Brigham Young University where with my junior college associate degree from before my mission, I was able by August 1954 to complete my bachelor of arts degree with a major in accounting and a minor in Spanish.

By the end of my mission I realized that my involvement in scouting in Uruguay and its establishment in the mission, special young men who came into the Church because of our scouting activities, and special families like the Vinas family that my companions and I worked with and baptized were part of the reason my Heavenly Father wanted me to go to Uruguay.

Someone else could have done what I did, but my preparation as a youth before my mission made me the one Heavenly Father wanted to work to the advantage to His work and the Church to handle what was ripe for action in Uruguay and Paraguay. I doubt if any other mission in the world at that time would have been the right mission for me.

I firmly believe and testify that every missionary's call comes from God and is special to him or her as mine was to me.

Sources

Boy Scouts of America. *Scoutmaster's Handbook.* New Brunswick, N.J.: Boy Scouts of America, 1967.

Skinner, Rulon Dean. *Rulon Dean Skinner—A Personal History—Autobiography Volume I.* Provo, Utah: Rulon Dean Skinner, 1998.

The Church of Jesus Christ of Latter-day Saints. *For the Strength of Youth.* Salt Lake City: The Church of Jesus Christ of Latter-day Saints, 2001.

The Church of Jesus Christ of Latter-day Saints. *"Preach My Gospel": A Guide to Missionary Service.* Salt Lake City: The Church of Jesus Christ of Latter-day Saints, 2004.

ABOUT THE AUTHOR

Rulon Dean Skinner was born in Safford, Arizona, June 26, 1931, the son of Rulon Moroni Skinner and Violet Whipple Skinner. He completed two years at Gila Junior College (now Eastern Arizona College) at Thatcher, Arizona, graduating in 1950.

From 1950 to 1953, Rulon served a mission for The Church of Jesus Christ of Latter-day Saints in Uruguay. After his mission, he entered Brigham Young University and graduated with a bachelor's degree in accounting in August 1954. Rulon entered professional scouting with the Boy Scouts of America and served fifteen years in the Utah National Parks Council.

He became a member of the national staff of the Boy Scouts of America in the professional training division in September 1969 and was assigned to teach in the youth leadership department at Brigham Young University, which he did from 1969 to 1978. He earned a master's degree in recreation education from Brigham Young University in 1971.

Rulon severed professional ties with the Boy Scouts of America in 1978, remaining as a Brigham Young University instructor, then as assistant professor, and later as associate professor in the combined recreation management and youth leadership department until retirement in 1996.

In the Church, he has served in many positions, including as a member of a bishopric and a stake presidency, and as a branch president at the Missionary Training Center.

Rulon is married to the former Ruth Walters of Bridgeland, Utah. They have five children.